Advances in Pattern Recognition

Advances in Pattern Recognition is a series of books which brings together current developments in all areas of this multi-disciplinary topic. It covers both theoretical and applied aspects of pattern recognition, and provides texts for students and senior researchers.

Springer also publishes a related journal, **Pattern Analysis and Applications.** For more details see: http://springlink.com

This book series and journal are both edited by Professor Sameer Singh of Loughborough University, UK.

For other titles published in this series go to: www.springer.com

Bir Bhanu and Hui Chen

Human Ear Recognition by Computer

 Springer

Bir Bhanu, BS, MS, ME, EE, PhD
Center for Research in Intelligent Systems
University of California at Riverside
Riverside, California 92521
USA
bhanu@cris.ucr.edu

Hui Chen, BS, MS, PhD
Center for Research in Intelligent Systems
University of California at Riverside
Riverside, California 92521
USA
hchen@vislab.ucr.edu

Series Editor

Professor Sameer Singh
Research School of Informatics
Loughborough University
Loughborough
UK

Advances in Pattern Recognition Series ISSN 1617-7916
ISBN 978-1-84996-733-4   e-ISBN 978-1-84800-129-9
DOI 10.1007/978-1-84800-129-9

British Library Cataloguing in Publication Data
A catalogue record for this book is available from the British Library

Printed on acid-free paper.

9 8 7 6 5 4 3 2 1

Springer Science+Business Media
springer.com

Preface

Biometrics deals with recognition of individuals based on their physiological or behavioral characteristics. Researchers have done extensive biometric studies of fingerprints, faces, palm prints, irises and gaits. The Ear is a viable new class of biometrics with certain advantages over faces and fingerprints, which are the two most common biometrics in both academic research and industrial applications. For example, the ear is rich in features; it is a stable structure that does not change much with age and it does not change its shape with facial expressions. Furthermore, the ear is larger in size compared to fingerprints but smaller as compared to the face; and it can be easily captured from a distance without a fully cooperative subject, although sometimes it can be hidden with hair, or with a turban, muffler, scarf or earrings. The ear is made up of standard features like the face. These include the outer rim (helix) and ridges (anti-helix) parallel to the rim, the lobe, the concha (hollow part of ear) and the tragus (the small prominence of cartilage over the meatus).

Researchers have developed several biometrics techniques using 2D intensity images. The performance of these techniques is greatly affected by the pose variation and imaging conditions. However, an ear can be imaged in 3D using a range sensor that provides a registered color and range image pair. An example is shown on the cover of this book. A range image is relatively insensitive to illumination and contains surface shape information related to the anatomical structure, which makes it possible to develop robust 3D ear biometrics. This book explores all aspects of 3D ear recognition: representation, detection, recognition, indexing and performance prediction. The experimental results on the UCR (University of California at Riverside) dataset of 155 subjects with 902 images under pose variations and the University of Notre Dame dataset of 326 subjects with 700 images with time-lapse gallery-probe pairs are presented to compare and demonstrate the effectiveness of proposed algorithms and systems.

The book describes complete human recognition systems using 3D ear biometrics. It also presents various algorithms that will be of significant interest to students, engineers, scientists and application developers involved in basic and applied research in the areas of biometrics and 3D object recognition.

Specific algorithms addressed in the book include:

- *Ear Helix/Anti-Helix Based Representation:* This effective approach consists of two steps and uses registered 2D color and range images for locating the ear helix and the anti-helix. In the *first step* a skin color classifier is used to isolate the side face in an image by modeling the skin color and non–skin color distributions as a mixture of Gaussians. The edges from the 2D color image are combined with the step edges from the range image to locate regions-of-interest (ROIs) which may contain an ear. In the *second step*, to locate an ear accurately, the reference 3D ear shape model, which is represented by a set of discrete 3D vertices on the ear helix and the anti-helix parts, is adapted to individual ear images by following a new global-to-local registration procedure instead of training an active shape model built from a large set of ears to learn the shape variation.
- *Global-to-Local Registration:* This approach for ear detection is followed to build a database of ears that belong to different people. Initially an estimate of the the global registration is obtained. This is followed by the local deformation process where it is necessary to preserve the structure of the reference ear shape model since neighboring points cannot move independently under the deformation due to physical constraints. The bending energy of thin plate spline, a quantitative measure for non-rigid deformations, is incorporated into the proposed optimization formulation as a regularization term to preserve the topology of the ear shape model under the shape deformation. The optimization procedure drives the initial global registration towards the ear helix and the anti-helix parts, which results in one-to-one correspondence of the ear helix and the anti-helix between the reference ear shape model and the input image.
- *Ear Recognition Using Helix/Anti-Helix Representation:* In order to estimate the initial rigid transformation between a gallery-probe pair, the correspondence of ear helix and anti-helix parts available from the ear detection algorithm between a gallery-probe ear pair is established and is used to compute the initial rigid transformation. This transformation is then applied to randomly selected control points of the hypothesized gallery ear in the database. A modified iterative closest point (ICP) algorithm is run to improve the transformation that brings a gallery ear and a probe ear into the best alignment, for every gallery-probe pair. The root mean square (RMS) registration error is used as the matching error criterion. The subject in the gallery with the minimum RMS error is declared as the recognized person in the probe image.
- *Ear Recognition Using a New Local Surface Patch Representation:* For the local surface patch (LSP) representation, a local surface descriptor is characterized by a centroid, a local surface type, and a 2D histogram. The local surface descriptors are computed for the feature points which are defined as either the local minimum or the local maximum of shape indexes. By comparing the local surface patches for a gallery and a probe image, the potential corresponding local surface patches are established and then filtered by geometric constraints. Based on the filtered correspondences, the initial rigid transformation is estimated. Now a procedure

similar to that used with helix/anti-helix representation is used to recognize the probe ear.

- *Efficient Ear Indexing and Recognition:* This book introduces a novel computational framework for rapid recognition of 3D ears. This framework combines the feature embedding and the support vector machine (SVM) technique to rank the hypotheses. No assumptions about the distributions of features is made, and the performance of the proposed algorithm is scalable with the database size without sacrificing much accuracy.
- *Performance Prediction for 3D Ear Recognition:* The book presents a binomial model to predict the ear recognition performance on large datasets by modeling cumulative match characteristic (CMC) curve as a binomial distribution.
- *Generality and Applications:* This book presents applications of (a) LSP representation to general 3D object recognition in range image and (b) global-to-local shape registration to binary and grayscale images obtained from various applications.

Three-dimensional ear recognition is a relatively new area in biometrics research. Our research into recognizing people by their ears started out with curiosity and interest since the ear is rich in 3D features. This research led to the first publication in the field on 3D ear recognition in the Multi-Modal User Authentication (MMUA) Workshop at the University of California at Santa Barbara in 2003. At that time, we had a database of only 10 subjects. Since then, we have compiled our own data collection (the UCR dataset) of 902 pairs of images of 155 subjects. An ear database was also collected at the University of Notre Dame (the UND dataset). We also have a dataset of 326 subjects with 700 images that was available to us from the UND dataset. This book shows the results on both the UCR and the UND datasets. The authors would like to thank Dr. Kevin Bowyer, Dr. Ping Yan, and Dr. Patrick Flynn for providing the database that has been used in the book.

We would like to thank Mark Burge and Wilhelm Burger for the use of Figure 13.1(b) from Chapter 13, Ear Biometrics in *Biometrics: Personal Identification in Networked Society*, edited by A. Jain, R. Bolle and S. Pankanti, Kluwer Academic Publishers, Boston, 1999.

We would like to acknowledge ARO support as we conducted our research. We would also like to thank Wayne Wheeler at Springer for his interest and encouragement and Catherine Brett for keeping us close to the schedule.

Riverside, California, USA,   *Bir Bhanu and Hui Chen*
October 1, 2007

Contents

List of Tables

List of Figures

1

Introduction

"The ear, thanks to these multiple small valleys and hills which furrow across it, is the most significant factor from the point of view of identification. Immutable in its form since birth, resistant to the influences of environment and education, this organ remains, during the entire life, like the intangible legacy of heredity and of the intrauterine life."

A. Bertillon, 1890 [5, 6].

1.1 Ear Biometrics and History

Biometrics deal with recognition of individuals based on their physiological or behavioral characteristics [7]. Since the characteristics for each human are distinct and unique, biometrics provide a more reliable system than the other traditional systems, such as identity cards, keys, and passwords. Researchers have done extensive biometric studies on fingerprints, faces, palm prints, irises and gaits. Ear biometrics, on the other hand, has received scant attention.

In claiming the ear as a class of biometrics, we have to show that it is viable as a class of biometrics (i.e., universality, uniqueness, and permanence [7]). After decades of research of anthropometric measurements of ear photographs of thousands of people, Iannarelli has found that no two ears are alike, even in the cases of identical and fraternal twins, triplets, and quadruplets [8]. He has also found that the structure of the ear does not change radically over time.

Iannarelli has appeared personally as an expert witness in many court cases [6]. In the preface of his book [8], Iannarelli says:

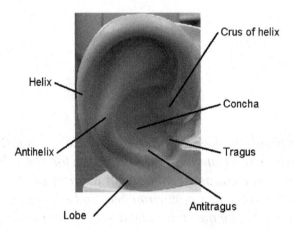

Fig. 1.1. The external ear and its anatomical parts.

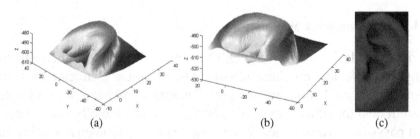

Fig. 1.2. Range image and color image captured by a Minolta Vivid 300 camera. In images (a) and (b), the range image of one ear is displayed as the shaded mesh from two viewpoints (The units of x, y and z are in millimeters). Image (c) shows the color image of the ear.

Through 38 years of research and application in earology, the author has found that in literally thousands of ears that were examined by visual means, photographs, ear prints, and latent ear print impressions, no two ears were found to be identical—not even the ears of any one individual. This uniqueness held true in cases of identical and fraternal twins, triplets, and quadruplets.

By the statement "no two ears were found to be identical—not even the ears of any one individual," we understand and find based on our own analysis and results presented in this book, that the variations between the ear signatures of an individual are significantly less than the variations among different people. This is the scientific basis for considering the ear as a class of biometrics.

The anatomical structure of the human ear is shown in Figure 1.1. These include the outer rim (helix) and ridges (anti-helix) parallel to the helix, the lobe, the concha (hollow part of ear) and the tragus (the small prominence of cartilage over the meatus). The crus of helix is the beginning of helix.

1.2 2D and 3D Ear Biometrics

Researchers have developed several biometric techniques using the 2D intensity images of human ears [7, Chap. 13] [9–11]. The performance of these techniques is greatly affected by the pose variation and imaging conditions. However, an ear can be imaged in 3D using a range sensor which provides a registered color and range image. Figure 1.2 shows an example of a range image and the registered color image acquired by a Minolta Vivid 300 camera. A range image is relatively insensitive to illuminations and contains surface shape information related to the anatomical structure, which makes it possible to develop a robust 3D ear biometrics. Examples of ear recognition using 3D data are [1, 12–19].

1.3 3D Ear Databases

The experiments were performed on the dataset collected by us (the UCR dataset) and the University of Notre Dame public dataset (the

UND dataset).[1] In the UCR dataset there is no time lapse between the gallery and probe for the same subject, while there is a time lapse of a few weeks (on the average) in the UND dataset.

1.3.1 The UCR Dataset

The data are captured by a Minolta Vivid 300 camera which is shown in Figure 1.3. This camera uses the light-stripe method to emit a horizontal stripe light to the object and the reflected light is then converted by triangulation into distance information. The camera outputs a range image and its registered color image in less than one second. The range image contains 200×200 grid points and each grid point has a 3D coordinate (x, y, z) and a set of color (r, g, b) values. During the acquisition, 155 subjects sit on a chair about 0.55–0.75 m from the camera in an indoor office environment. The first shot is taken when a subject's left-side face is approximately parallel to the image plane; two shots are taken when the subject is asked to rotate his/her head to the left and to the right side within $\pm 35°$ with respect to his/her torso. During this process, there can be some face tilt as well, which is not measured. A total of six images per subject are recorded. A total of 902 shots are used for the experiments since some shots are not properly recorded. Every person has at least four shots. The average number of points on the side face scans is 23,205. There are there different poses in the collected data: frontal, left, and right. Among the total 155 subjects, there are 17 females. Among the 155 subjects, 6 subjects have earrings and 12 subjects have their ears partially occluded by hair (with less than 10% occlusion). Figure 1.4 shows side face range images and the corresponding color images of six people collected in our database. The pose variations, the earrings, and the hair occlusions can be clearly seen in this figure.

1.3.2 The UND Dataset

The data are acquired with a Minolta Vivid 910 camera. The camera outputs a 480×640 range image and its registered color image of the same size. During acquisition, the subject sits approximately 1.5 m away from the sensor with the left side of the face toward the camera.

---

[1] http://www.nd.edu/~cvrl/UNDBiometricsDatabase.html, Collection F and a subset of Collection G

Fig. 1.3. The Minolta Vivid 300.

In Collection F, there are 302 subjects with 302 time-lapse gallery-probe pairs. Figure 1.5 shows side face range images and the corresponding color images of two people from this collection. Collection G contains 415 subjects of which 302 subjects are from Collection F. The most important part of Collection G is that it has 24 subjects with images taken at four different viewpoints. We perform experiments only on these 24 subjects and not the *entire* Collection G because Collection G became available only very recently and contains the entire Collection F that we have already used in our experiments.

1.4 Major Ideas Presented in the Book

This book presents the following important ideas in ear biometrics, especially 3D ear biometrics.

- Develops automatic human recognition systems using 3D ear biometrics.
- Presents a two-step procedure for the accurate localization of an ear in a given image using a single reference ear shape model and fusion of color and range images. Adapts the reference shape model

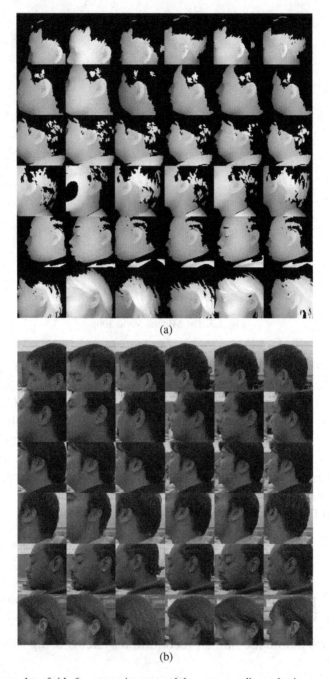

(a)

(b)

Fig. 1.4. Examples of side face range images and the corresponding color images for six people in our dataset. (a) Range images. (b) Color images. Note the pose variations, the earrings and the hair occlusions for the six shots.

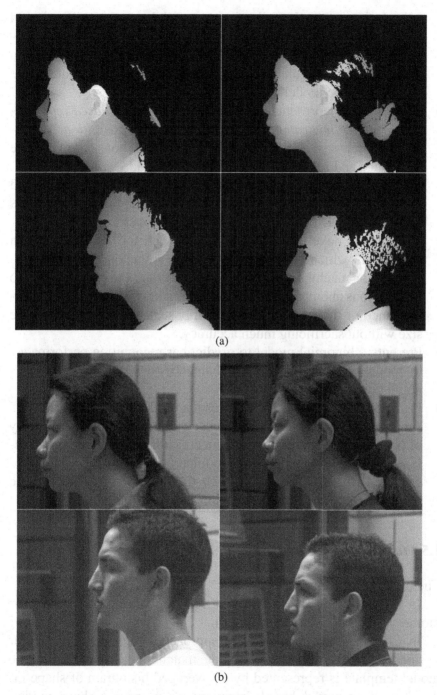

Fig. 1.5. Examples of side face range images and the corresponding color images for two people in the UND dataset Collection F. (a) Range images. (b) Color images. In (a) and (b) the left column shows the gallery images and the right column shows the probe images.

to incoming images by following a new global-to-local registration procedure with an associated optimization formulation. Incorporates the bending energy of thin plate spline into the optimization formulation as a regularization term to preserve the structure of the reference shape model under the deformation.

- Proposes two representations: the *helix/anti-helix based representation* and the *invariant local surface patch representation*, for recognizing ears in 3D. Evaluates these representations for their pose invariance and robustness to the real world data.
- Introduces a simple and effective surface matching scheme based on the modified iterative closest point (ICP) algorithm. Initializes ICP by a full 3D (translation and rotation) transformation.
- Introduces a novel computational framework for rapid recognition of 3D ears which combines the feature embedding and the support vector machine (SVM) technique to rank the hypotheses. No assumptions about the distributions of features is made and the performance of the proposed algorithm is scalable with the database size without sacrificing much accuracy.
- Presents a binomial model to predict ear recognition performance by modeling cumulative match characteristic (CMC) curve as a binomial distribution.
- Demonstrates the experimental results on the UCR dataset of 155 subjects with 902 images under pose variations and the University of Notre Dame dataset of 302 subjects with 604 images with time-lapse gallery-probe pairs. It also compares with the other published work [14–19]. In addition, it shows the results on 24 subjects (the UND dataset Collection G) taken from four different viewpoints.

1.5 Organization of the Book

The book consists of nine chapters.

In Chapter 2, we give a review of related work in the fields of ear biometrics and 3D object recognition.

In Chapter 3, we present three approaches for localizing the ear in side face range images: (1) template matching based–detection: the model template is represented by an averaged histogram of shape index. (2) shape model–based detection: we propose a shape model-based technique for locating human ears. The ear shape model is represented by a set of discrete 3D vertices corresponding to ear helix and anti-helix parts. (3) global-to-local registration–based detection. We use a two-step approach for human ear detection by locating ear helix and anti-helix parts in registered 2D color and range images. Instead of training an active shape model to learn the shape variation, the ear shape model is adapted to images by following the global-to-local registration procedure.

In Chapter 4, we propose an ear helix/anti-helix representation for matching surfaces in 3D. The 3D coordinates of the ear helix/anti-helix are obtained from the detection algorithm described in Chapter 3. The correspondences of ear helix and anti-helix parts are used to obtain an initial transformation between every gallery-probe ear pair. This transformation is applied to randomly selected locations of gallery ears and a modified ICP algorithm is used to iteratively refine the transformation to bring the gallery ear and the probe ear into the best alignment. The root mean square (RMS) registration error is used as the matching error criterion. The subject in the gallery with the minimum RMS error is declared as the recognized person in the probe image.

In Chapter 5, we propose a novel surface descriptor, local surface patch (LSP) representation for recognizing human ears in 3D. A local surface descriptor is characterized by a centroid, a local surface type, and a 2D histogram. The 2D histogram shows the frequency of occurrence of shape index values versus the angle between the normal of reference feature point and that of its neighbors. Comparing local surface descriptors between a probe and a gallery image, an initial correspondence of local surface patches is established which is then filtered by geometric constraints. This generates a set of hypotheses for verification. The final verification is achieved by estimating transformations and aligning gallery images with the probe image based on the ICP algorithm.

In Chapter 6, we present a novel method for rapid recognition of 3D ears which combines the feature embedding for the fast retrieval of surface descriptors and the support vector machine (SVM) learning technique for ranking the hypotheses to generate a short list for the verification. The local surface patch (LSP) representation is used to find the correspondences between a gallery-probe pair. Due to the high dimensionality and the large number of LSP descriptors, the *FastMap* embedding algorithm maps the feature vectors to a low-dimensional space where the distance relationships are preserved. A K-d tree algorithm works in the low-dimensional space for fast retrieval of similar descriptors. The initial correspondences are filtered and grouped to remove false correspondences using geometric constraints. Based on the correspondences, a set of features is computed as a measure of the similarity between the gallery-probe pair, and then the similarities are ranked using the support vector machines (SVM) rank learning algorithm to generate a short list of candidate models for verification.

In Chapter 7, we present a binomial model to predict ear recognition performance. Match and non-match distances are used to estimate the distributions. By modeling cumulative match characteristic (CMC) curve as a binomial distribution, the ear recognition performance is predicted on a larger gallery.

In Chapter 8, we apply the proposed techniques to the general 3D object recognition and non-rigid shape registration. The LSP representation proposed in Chapter 5 is general and can be used to recognize general 3D objects in range images. The global-to-local registration with an optimization formulation proposed in Chapter 3 is used to handle non-rigid 2D shape registration.

In Chapter 9, we present a summary of the book and the future work.

Ear Detection and Recognition in 2D and 3D

Although in the field of computer vision and pattern recognition ear biometrics has received scant attention compared to the popular biometrics such as face and fingerprint, ear biometrics has played a significant role in forensic science and its use by law enforcement agencies for many years. Iannarelli [8] developed the famous ear classification system based on manual anthropometric measurements of ear photographs of thousands of people. The "Iannarelli system" is based upon 12 measurements illustrated in Figure 2.1. The locations shown are measured from specially aligned and normalized photographs of the right ear. This system has been in use for more than 40 years, although the reliability of this earprint-based system has recently been challenged in court [20, 21].

All the work described in the previous paragraphs was done manually. Rutty et al. [22] considered how Iannarelli's techniques might be automated. Meijermana et al. [23], in a European initiative, have looked into the value of earprints for forensics.

The early research on automated ear recognition was focused on 2D intensity images. However, the performance of these systems is greatly affected by imaging conditions. It is possible to image an ear in 3D. The 3D data collected by a range sensor provides geometric shape information that is relatively insensitive to illuminations. Design of a biometrics system based on 3D data has been proposed in recent years. Furthermore, the ear can be thought of as a rigid free-form object. Therefore, in this chapter the related work is reviewed in several areas: 2D ear biometrics, 3D biometrics, and 3D object recognition.

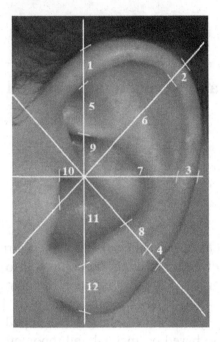

Fig. 2.1. Twelve anthropometric measurements in "Iannarelli system." This figure is taken from [7, Chap. 13].

2.1 2D Ear Biometrics

Burge and Burger [9] developed a computer vision system to recognize ears in the intensity images. Their algorithm consists of four components: edge extraction, curve extraction, construction of a graph model from the Voronoi diagram of the edge segments, and graph matching. Hurley et al. [10, 24] applied a force field transform to the entire ear images and extracted wells and channels. The wells and channels form the basis of an ear's signature. To evaluate differences among ears, they used a measure of the average normalized distance of the well positions, together with the accumulated direction to the position of each well point from a chosen reference point.

Victor et al. [25] used principal component analysis on ear and face images and evaluated the face and ear biometrics. Tests were performed with different gallery/probe combinations, such as probes of ears on the same day but with different ears, or probes of faces on a different day but with similar facial expression. Their results showed that the 2D face image is a more reliable biometrics than the 2D ear image. Chang et al. [11] also used principal component analysis for ear and face images and performed experiments with face, ear, and face plus ear. Their results showed that multimodal recognition using both face and ear achieved a much better performance than the individual biometrics.

Abdel-Mottaleb and Zhao [26] developed a system for ear recognition from profile images of the face. They used force field transformation for ear feature extraction. Yuan et al. [27] used face profile and ear for human recognition. Mu et al. [28] proposed long–axis based shape features for ear recognition. Yuan et al. [29] proposed and improved non-negative matrix factorization with sparseness constraints for occluded ear recognition. Because the PCA-based approach is sensitive to the slightest rotation during image acquisition process, Abate et al. [30] presented rotation invariant Fourier descriptors for feature extraction and recognition. Zhang et al. [31] developed an approach that combined independent component analysis (ICA) and radial-based functions (RBF) network for ear recognition. Chora et al. [32] presented a geometric method for feature extraction from contours of an ear image and used them for recognition. Pun and Mu [33] provided an overview and comparison of the ear and other biometrics.

The performance of all these 2D approaches is significantly lower than the 3D approaches for ear recognition that are presented in this book [11, 34].

2.2 3D Biometrics

Detection and recognition are the two major components of a biometrics system. In the following, we first present the related work on object detection and then on object recogntion.

2.2.1 Biometrics Object Detection

Chen and Bhanu [35] proposed a template matching–based detection for locating ear regions in side face range images. The model template is represented by an averaged histogram of the shape index values. The detection is a four-step procedure: (i) step edge detection and thresholding, (ii) image dilation, (iii) connected-component labeling, and (iv) template matching.

Chen and Bhanu [36] developed a shape model-based technique for more accurately locating human ears in side face range images. The ear shape model is represented by a set of discrete 3D vertices on the ear helix and anti-helix parts. By aligning the ear shape model with the range images, the ear can be detected, and the ear helix and anti-helix parts are identified. Chen and Bhanu [1] developed a two-step approach for precisely locating human ears in side face range images by fusion of color/range images and adaptation of a reference 3D ear shape model.

Boehnen and Russ [37] proposed an algorithm to utilize the combination of the range and registered color images for automatically identifying facial features. The foreground is first segmented using the range data and then the skin color detection is used to identify potential skin pixels, which are further refined using Z-based range erosion to compute the eye and mouth maps. Finally, the geometric-based confidence of candidates is computed to aid in the selection of best feature set.

Tsalakanidou et al. [38] introduced a face localization procedure that combines both depth and color data. First, the human body is easily separated from the background by using the depth information and its geometric structure; and then the head and torso are identified by modeling the 3D point distribution as a mixture model of two Gaussians; finally, the position of the face is further refined using the color images by exploiting the symmetric structure of the face.

Lu et al. [39] used the shape index to identify the inside of the eye and to locate the nose using the depth information. Yan and Bowyer [2, 19] proposed an active contour-based segmentation using range and color images for the localization of ear in a side face range image.

2.2.2 Biometrics Object Recognition

Lee and Milios [40] developed an algorithm for finding corresponding convex regions between two face range images. Each convex region is represented by its extended Gaussian image (EGI). By correlating EGIs, a similarity function between two regions is calculated. Further, a graph matching algorithm is run to find the optimal correspondence.

Gordon [41] presented a face recognition system based on the range data of faces. Geometric features, calculated on salient surfaces such as eyes, nose, and head, form face descriptors. The comparison between two faces is performed by using the Euclidean distance measure in the scaled feature space formed by the face descriptors. Experiments with a database of 24 faces showed 80%–100% recognition rate even with a small feature set and simple statistical classification methods.

Chua [42] used the point signature representation of 3D range data of the face for the registration of two face surfaces with different facial expressions. From the registration results, the rigid parts of the face are identified as those regions that had low registration errors. Therefore, the 3D non-rigid face recognition problem is reduced to the rigid case.

Bronstein et al. [43] introduced a representation invariant to isometric deformation of 3D faces. Given a polyhedral approximation of the facial surface, the bending-invariant canonical form is computed, which allows mapping 2D facial texture images into special images that incorporate the 3D geometry of the face. Experiments with a 3D database of 157 subjects are shown to outperform the 2D eigenface-based approach.

Chang et al. [44] presented a PCA-based approach to do face recognition using multiple sensors (CCD and range sensor). Experimental results showed that a multi-modal rank-one recognition rate is higher than using either a 2D or a 3D modality alone. Chang et al. [45] presented an experimental study in multimodal 2D+3D face recognition using the PCA-based methods. Experiments showed that multimodality of 2D and 3D and multi-image representation for a person in both the gallery and probe set improved face recognition performance.

Lu [46] presented a face recognition system which integrated 3D face models with 2D appearance images. The recognition engine has two components: 3D surface matching using a modified ICP algorithm and constrained appearance-based matching using linear discriminant analysis. The scores obtained by the two matching components are combined using the weighted sum rule to make the final decision.

Bhanu and Chen [1, 12] proposed a local surface patch (LSP) descriptor for recognizing humans by their ears in 3D. LSP is defined by a centroid, its surface type, and a 2D histogram of shape index versus the angle between surface normals of a reference feature point and its local neighbors. Experiments with a dataset of 10 subjects are shown. Chen and Bhanu [13] introduced a two-step ICP algorithm for matching 3D ears. In the first step a coarse match was obtained by aligning a model ear helix with the test ear helix; in the second step ICP iteratively refined the transformation computed in the first step to bring the model ear and the test ear into best alignment.

Yan and Bowyer [2, 14–19, 34, 47] applied 3D principal component analysis, 3D edge-based, and ICP-based registration techniques to 3D ear images, and also applied 2D PCA to 2D ear images. They performed experiments on a database of about 400 persons and used different fusion rules for combining 2D and 3D ear biometrics.

2.3 3D Object Recognition

3D object recognition is an important research field of computer vision and pattern recognition. In this book, we discuss the problem of recognizing 3D objects from 3D range images. Specifically, given a 3D test range image, the task of recognition is to identify objects in the test range image by comparing them to the objects saved in the model database and estimate their poses. In the early years of 3D computer vision, the representation schemes included wire-frame, constructive solid geometry (CSG), extended Gaussian image (EGI), generalized cylinders, planar faces [48], and superquadric [49, 50]. All of these are not suitable for representing free-from surfaces. The ear can be thought of as a rigid free-form object. Researchers have proposed various local surface descriptors for recognizing 3D free-form objects. A comprehensive survey on 3D free-form object recognition can be found in [51].

2.3.1 3D Object Recognition Using Surface Signatures

Stein and Medioni [52] used two different types of primitives: 3D curves and splashes, for representation and matching. 3D curves are obtained from edges and they correspond to the discontinuity in depth and orientation. For smooth areas, splash is defined by surface normals along contours of different radii. Both of the primitives can be encoded by a set of 3D super segments, which are described by the curvature and torsion angles of a super segment. 3D super segments are indexed into a hash table for fast retrieval and matching. Hypotheses are generated by casting votes to the hash table, and bad hypotheses are removed by estimating rigid transformations. Chua and Jarvis [53] used the point signature representation, which describes the structural neighborhood of a point, to represent 3D free-form objects. Point signature is a 1-D signed distance profile with respect to the rotation angle defined by the angle between the normal vector of the point on the curve and the reference vector. Recognition is performed by matching the signatures of points on the scene surfaces to those of points on the model surfaces. The maximum and minimum values of the signatures were used as indexes to a 2D table for fast retrieval and matching.

Johnson and Hebert [3] presented the spin image (SI) representation for range images. Given an oriented point on a 3D surface, its shape is described by two parameters: (i) distance to the tangent plane of the oriented point from its neighbors and (ii) the distance to the normal vector of the oriented point. The approach involves three steps: generation of spin image, finding of corresponding points and verification.

First, spin images are calculated at every vertex of the model surfaces. Then the corresponding point pair is found by computing the correlation coefficient of two spin images centered at those two points. Next, the corresponding pairs are filtered by using geometric constraints. Finally, a rigid transformation is computed and a modified iterative closest point (ICP) algorithm is used for verification. In order to speed up the matching process, principal component analysis (PCA) is used to compress spin images. Correa et al. [4] proposed the spherical spin image (SSI) which maps the spin image to points onto a unit sphere. Corresponding points are found by computing the angle between two SSIs. Yamany et al. [54] introduced the surface signature representation which is also a 2D histogram. One parameter is the distance between the center point and every surface point. The other parameter is the angle between the normal of the center point and every surface point. Signature matching is done by template matching.

Zhang and Hebert [55] introduced harmonic shape images (HSI) which are 2D representation of 3D surface patches. HSIs are unique and they preserve the shape and continuity of the underlying surfaces. Surface matching is simplified to matching harmonic shape images. Sun and Abidi [56] introduced the 3D point's "fingerprint" representation which is a set of 2D contours formed by the projection of geodesic circles onto the tangent plane. Each point's fingerprint carries information of the normal variation along geodesic circles. Corresponding points are found by comparing the fingerprints of points.

Chen and Bhanu [57] used the local surface patch representation [12] to 3D free-form object recognition. Correspondence and candidate models are hypothesized by comparing local surface patches. In order to speed up the search process and deal with a large set of objects, local surface patches were indexed into a hash table.

2.3.2 Rapid 3D Object Recognition

Although various techniques have been proposed for 3D object recognition, most of them focus on the recognition of 3D dissimilar objects in a small database.

Mokhtarian et al. [58] introduced an algorithm to recognize free-from 3D objects based on the geometric hashing and global verification. Given a scene, the feature points were extracted and matched to those saved in the hash table built in the offline stage. Then the global verification was performed to select the most likely candidates. The experimental results on 20 objects were presented.

Stein and Medioni [52] presented an approach for the recognition of 3D objects using two types of primitives: 3D curves and splashes, for representation and matching. 3D curves were obtained from edges and they correspond to the discontinuity in depth and orientation. For smooth areas, splash was defined by surface normals along contours of different radii. The 3D super segments were indexed into a hash table for fast retrieval and matching. Hypotheses were generated by casting votes to the hash table and bad hypotheses were removed by estimating rigid transformations. The experimental results on nine objects were presented.

Chua and Jarvis [53] introduced the point signature representation which was a 1D signed distance profile with respect to the rotation angle. Recognition was performed by matching the signatures of points on the scene surfaces to those of points on the model surfaces. The maximum and minimum values of the signatures were used as indexes to a 2D table for fast retrieval and matching. The experimental results on 15 objects were presented.

Yi and Chelberg [59] developed a Bayesian framework to achieve efficient indexing of model objects. The hypotheses were generated and verified for features detected in a scene in the order of the discriminatory power of these feature for model objects. The experimental results on 20 objects were presented.

Johnson and Hebert [3] presented the spin image (SI) representation for surface matching. Given an oriented point on a 3D surface, its shape was described by two parameters: (i) distance to the tangent plane of the oriented point from its neighbors and (ii) the distance to the normal vector of the oriented point. In order to speed up searching the closest spin images, principal component analysis (PCA) was used to compress the spin images. The experimental results on 20 objects were presented.

Chen and Bhanu [57] introduced an integrated local surface patch (LSP) descriptor for surface representation and object recognition. A local surface descriptor was defined by a centroid, its surface type, and 2D histogram. In order to speed up the search process and deal with a large set of objects, model local surface patches were indexed into a hash table. Given a set of test local surface patches, the potential corresponding local surface patches and candidate models are hypothesized by casting votes for models containing similar surface descriptors. The experimental results for nine objects were presented.

2.4 Conclusions

In this chapter, we presented an overview of the research work that has been carried out for manual ear identification and automatic 2D and 3D ear recognition. We have also provided an overview of 3D biometrics, 3D object recognition, and 3D indexing techniques for rapid object recognition. In the following chapters, we present in-depth details of 3D ear detection, 3D ear recognition, 3D ear indexing, and 3D ear performance characterization.

3D Ear Detection from Side Face Range Images

Human ear detection is the first task of a human ear recognition system and its performance significantly affects the overall quality of the system. In this chapter, we propose three techniques for locating human ears in side face range images: template matching based detection, ear shape model based detection, and fusion of color and range images and global-to-local registration based detection. The first two approaches only use range images, and the third approach fuses the color and range images.

3.1 3D Ear Detection Using Only Range Images

The template matching based approach [35] has two stages: offline model template building and online ear detection. The ear can be thought of as a rigid object with much concave and convex areas. The averaged histogram of shape index represents the ear model template since shape index is a quantitative measure of the shape of a surface. During the online detection, we first perform the step edge computation and thresholding since there is a sharp step edge around the ear boundary, and then we do image dilation and connected-component analysis to find the potential regions containing an ear. Next, for every potential region, we grow the region and compute the dissimilarity between each region's histogram of shape indexes and the model template. Finally, among all of the regions, we choose the one with the minimum dissimilarity as the detected region that contains ear.

For the second approach, the ear shape model is represented by a set of discrete 3D vertices corresponding to ear helix and anti-helix parts

[36]. Since the two curves formed by the ear helix and anti-helix parts are similar for different people, we do not take into account the small deformation of two curves between different persons, which greatly simplifies our ear shape model. Given side face range images, first the step edges are extracted; then the edge segments are dilated, thinned and grouped into different clusters which are the potential regions containing an ear. For each cluster, we register the ear shape model with the edges. The region with the minimum mean registration error is declared as the detected ear region; the ear helix and anti-helix parts are identified in this process.

3.1.1 Template Matching Based Detection

Shape Index

Shape index S_i, a quantitative measure of the shape of a surface at a point p, is defined by (3.1),

$$S_i(p) = \frac{1}{2} - \frac{1}{\pi}\tan^{-1}\frac{k_1(p) + k_2(p)}{k_1(p) - k_2(p)} \tag{3.1}$$

where k_1 and k_2 are maximum and minimum principal curvatures, respectively [60]. With this definition, all shapes can be mapped into the interval $S_i \in [0, 1]$. The shape categories and corresponding shape index ranges are listed in Table 3.1. From the table, we can see that larger shape index values represent convex surfaces and smaller shape index values represent concave surfaces.

Table 3.1. Surface shape categories and the range of shape index values.

Shape category		S_i range
Spherical cup		[0, 1/16)
Trough		[1/16, 3/16)
Rut		[3/16, 5/16)
Saddle rut		[5/16, 7/16)
Saddle		[7/16, 9/16)
Saddle ridge		[9/16, 11/16)
Ridge		[11/16, 13/16)
Dome		[13/16, 15/16)
Spherical cap		[15/16, 1]

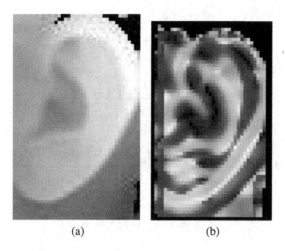

         (a)   (b)

Fig. 3.1. (a) Ear range image. Darker pixels are away from the camera and the lighter ones are closer. (b) Its shape index image. The darker pixels correspond to concave surfaces and the lighter ones correspond to convex surfaces.

The ear has significant convex and concave areas, which gives us a hint to use the shape index for ear detection. The original ear range image and its shape index image are shown in Figure 3.1. In Figure 3.1(b), the brighter pixels denote large shape index values which correspond to ridge and dome surfaces. The ridge and valley areas form a pattern for ear detection. We use the distribution of shape index as a robust and compact descriptor since 2D shape index image is much too detailed. The histogram h can be calculated by $h(k) = \#\ of\ points\ with\ shape\ index\ \in bin(k)$. The histogram is normalized during the implementation.

Curvature Estimation

In order to estimate curvatures, we fit a biquadratic surface (3.2) to a local window and use the least squares method to estimate the parameters of the quadratic surface, and then use differential geometry to calculate the surface normal, Gaussian and mean curvatures and principal curvatures [49, 61]. Based on differential geometry, surface normal **n**, Gaussian curvature K, mean curvature H, principal curvatures $k_{1,2}$ are given by (3.3), (3.4), (3.5) and (3.6), respectively:

$$f(x, y) = ax^2 + by^2 + cxy + dx + ey + f \qquad (3.2)$$

$$\mathbf{n} = \frac{(-f_x, -f_y, 1)}{\sqrt{1 + f_x^2 + f_y^2}} \tag{3.3}$$

$$K = \frac{f_{xx}f_{yy} - f_{xy}^2}{(1 + f_x^2 + f_y^2)^2} \tag{3.4}$$

$$H = \frac{f_{xx} + f_{yy} + f_{xx}f_y^2 + f_{yy}f_x^2 - 2f_x f_y f_{xy}}{2(1 + f_x^2 + f_y^2)^{1.5}} \tag{3.5}$$

$$k_{1,2} = H \pm \sqrt{H^2 - K} \tag{3.6}$$

Model Template Building

Given a set of training side face range images, first we extract ears in each of the images manually and then calculate its shape index image and histogram the shape index image. After we get the histograms for each training image, we average the histograms and use the averaged histogram as our model template. Figure 3.2 shows the model template, obtained using 20 training images, in which the two peaks correspond to the convex and concave regions of the ear, respectively.

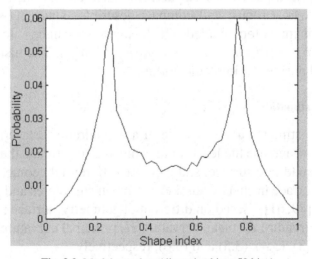

Fig. 3.2. Model template (discretized into 50 bins).

Step Edge Detection, Thresholding, and Dilation

There is a sharp change in depth around the ear helix part, which is helpful in identifying the ear region. Given a side face range image, the step edge magnitude, denoted by I_{step}, is calculated. I_{step} is defined by the maximum distance in depth between the center pixel and its neighbors in a $w \times w$ window. I_{step} can be written as:

$$I_{\text{step}}(i,j) = \max|z(i,j) - z(i+k,j+l)|,$$
$$-(w-1)/2 \leq k,l \leq (w-1)/2 \qquad (3.7)$$

where w is the width of the window and $z(i,j)$ is the z coordinate of the point (i,j). To get the step edge magnitude image, a $w \times w$ window is translated over the original side face range image and the maximum distance calculated from (3.7) replaces the pixel value of the pixel covered by the center of the window. The original side face range image and its step edge magnitude image are shown in Figure 3.3(a) and (b). From Figure 3.3(b), we clearly see that there is a sharp step edge around the ear boundary since brighter points denote large step edge magnitude.

The step edge image is thresholded to get a binary image which is shown in Figure 3.3(c). The threshold is set based on the maximum of I_{step}. Therefore, we can get a binary image by using (3.8),

$$F_T(i,j) = \begin{cases} 1 & \text{if } I_{\text{step}}(i,j) \geq \alpha * \max\{I_{\text{step}}\} \\ & 0 \leq \alpha \leq 1 \\ 0 & \text{otherwise} \end{cases} \qquad (3.8)$$

There are some holes in the thresholded binary image and we want to get the potential regions containing ears. We dilate the binary image to fill the holes. The dilated image is shown in Figure 3.3(d). There are some holes in the thresholded binary image and we would like to get the potential regions containing ears. We dilate the binary image to fill the holes using a 3×3 structuring element. The dilated image is shown in Figure 3.3(d).

Connected Component Labeling

Using the above result, we proceed to determine which regions can possibly contain human ears. To do so, we need to determine the

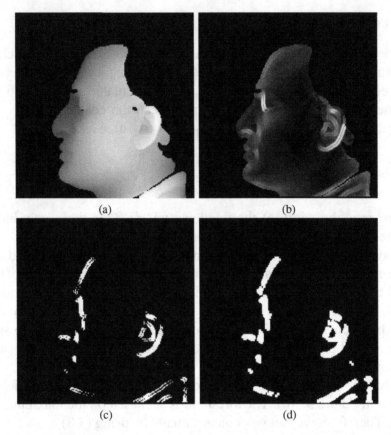

(a)   (b)

(c)   (d)

Fig. 3.3. (a) Original side face range image. (b) Step edge magnitude image. (c) Thresholded binary image. (d) Dilated image.

number of potential regions in the image. By running the connected component labeling algorithm, we can determine the number of regions. We used an 8-connected neighborhood to label a pixel. We remove smaller components whose area are less than β since the ear region is not small. The labeling result is shown in Figure 3.4(a) and the result after removing smaller components is shown in Figure 3.4(b).

After we get regions, we need to know their geometric properties such as the position and orientation. The position of a region may be defined using the center of the region. The center of area in binary images is the same as the center of the mass and it is computed as follows:

Fig. 3.4. (a) Labeled image. (b) Labeled image after removing smaller components.

$$\bar{x} = \frac{1}{A} \sum_{i=1}^{n} \sum_{j=1}^{m} j B[i,j], \quad \bar{y} = \frac{1}{A} \sum_{i=1}^{n} \sum_{j=1}^{m} i B[i,j] \qquad (3.9)$$

where B is $n \times m$ matrix representation of the binary region and A is the size of the region. For the orientation, we find the axis of elongation of the region. Along this axis the moment of the inertia will be the minimum. The axis is computed by finding the line for which the sum of the squared distances between region points and the line is minimum. The angle of θ is given by (3.10):

$$\theta = \frac{1}{2} \tan^{-1} \frac{b}{a-c} \qquad (3.10)$$

The parameters a, b and c are given by (3.11), (3.12), and (3.13), respectively.

$$a = \sum_{i=1}^{n} \sum_{j=1}^{m} (x'_{ij})^2 B[i,j] \qquad (3.11)$$

$$b = 2 \sum_{i=1}^{n} \sum_{j=1}^{m} x'_{ij} y'_{ij} B[i,j] \qquad (3.12)$$

$$c = \sum_{i=1}^{n} \sum_{j=1}^{m} (y'_{ij})^2 B[i,j] \qquad (3.13)$$

where $x' = x - \bar{x}$ and $y' = y - \bar{y}$. θ gives us a hint about the region growing direction.

Template Matching

As mentioned in Section 3.1.1, the model template is represented by an averaged histogram of shape index. Since a histogram can be thought of as an approximation of a probability distribution function, it is natural to use the $\chi^2 - divergence$ function (3.14) [62],

$$\chi^2(Q, V) = \sum_i \frac{(q_i - v_i)^2}{q_i + v_i} \tag{3.14}$$

where Q and V are normalized histograms. From (3.14), we know the dissimilarity is between 0 and 2. If the two histograms are exactly the same, the dissimilarity will be zero. If the two histograms do not overlap with each other, it will achieve the maximum value 2.

From Section 3.1.1, we get the potential regions that may contain the ears. For each region, we can find a minimum rectangular bounding box to include the region; then we grow the region based on the angle θ. If $0 \leq \theta \leq \pi/2$, we grow the rectangle by moving the top-right vertex right, up, and anti-diagonal, and then moving the bottom-left vertex left, down, and anti-diagonal. If $\pi/2 \leq \theta \leq \pi$, we grow the rectangle by moving the top-left vertex left, up, and diagonal, and then moving the bottom-right vertex right, down, and diagonal. For each region, we choose the grown rectangular box with the minimum dissimilarity as the candidate ear region. Finally, over all of the candidate regions, we select the one with the minimum dissimilarity as the detected ear region. We set a threshold γ for region growing, which controls the size of the region.

3.1.2 Reference Shape Model Based Ear Detection

Ear Shape Model Building

Considering the fact that the curves formed by ear helix and anti-helix parts are similar for different people, we construct the ear shape model from one person only. The reference ear shape model s is defined by 3D coordinates $\{x, y, z\}$ of n vertices which lie on the ear helix and the anti-helix parts. The ear helix and the anti-helix parts are manually marked for the reference shape model. The shape model s is represented by a $3n \times 1$ vector $(x_1, y_1, z_1, x_2, y_2, z_2, \cdots, x_n, y_n, z_n)^T$. Figure 3.5(a) shows the ear shape model s marked by the pluses (+). The corresponding color image is also shown in Figure 3.5(b).

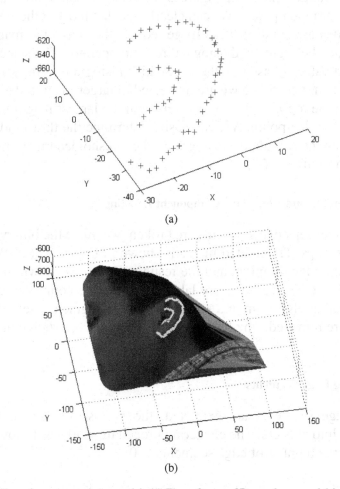

(a)

(b)

Fig. 3.5. The reference ear shape model. (a) The reference 3D ear shape model is displayed by the pluses (+). (b) Ear shape model is overlaid on the textured 3D face. The units of x, y and z are in mm.

Step Edge Detection and Thresholding

Given the step face range image, the step edge magnitude can be calculated as described in Section 3.1.1. One example of step edge magnitude image is shown in Figure 3.6. Figure 3.6(a) shows the original side face range image. In Figure 3.6(b), larger magnitudes are displayed as brighter pixels. We can clearly see that most of the step edge magnitudes are small values. To get edges, the step edge magnitude image must be segmented using a threshold operator. The selection of threshold value is based on the cumulative histogram of the step edge magnitude image. Since we are interested in larger magnitudes, in our approach the top $\eta\%$ ($\eta = 3.5$) pixels with the largest magnitudes are selected as edge points. We can easily determine the threshold by investigating the cumulative histogram. The thresholded binary image is shown in Figure 3.6(c).

Edge Thinning and Connected Component Labeling

Since some step edge segments are broken, we dilate the binary image to fill the gaps. The dilated image is shown in Figure 3.7(a). We proceed to do edge thinning, and the resulting image is shown in Figure 3.7(b). The edge segments are labeled by running connected component labeling algorithm and some small edge segments (less than 10 pixels) are removed. The left over edge segments are shown in Figure 3.7(c).

Clustering Edge Segments

After edge segments are extracted, those close to each other are grouped into clusters. The clustering procedure works as follows:
　　while the number of edge segments > 0

- $i = 0$
- Put the first edge segment e_i into a cluster C_i, and calculate its centroid $\{\mu_{xi}, \mu_{yi}\}$
- For all the other edge segments e_j
    - Calculate the centroid $\{\mu_{xj}, \mu_{yj}\}$
    - if $\max\{|\mu_{xj} - \mu_{xi}|, |\mu_{yj} - \mu_{yi}|\} \leq \epsilon$ put e_j into the cluster C_i, remove e_j and update the cluster's centroid.
- $i = i + 1$ and relabel the edge segments.

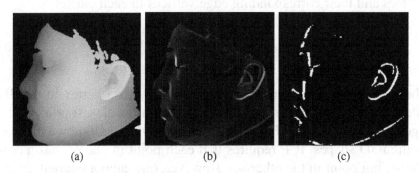

(a)   (b)   (c)

Fig. 3.6. (a) Original side face range image. (b) Step edge magnitude image. (c) Step edge image after thresholding.

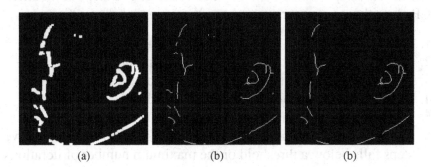

(a)   (b)   (b)

Fig. 3.7. (a) Dilated edge image. (b) Thinned edge image. (c) Left over edge segments.

Three examples of clustering results are shown in Figure 3.8. The first row of Figure 3.8 shows side face range images. The second row shows the corresponding clustering results where each cluster is bounded by a red rectangular box.

Locating Ears by Use of the Ear Shape Model

For each cluster obtained in the previous step, the problem of locating ears is to minimize the mean square error between the ear shape model vertices and their corresponding edge vertices in each cluster,

$$E = \frac{1}{n} \sum_{l=1}^{n} |T_r(s_i) - V(s_i)|^2 \tag{3.15}$$

where T_r is the rigid transformation and $V(s_i)$ is a vertex in the 3D side face image closest to the $T_r(s_i)$. The iterative closest point (ICP) algorithm developed by Besl and Mckay [63] is a well-known method to align 3D shapes. ICP requires that each point in one set has a corresponding point in the other set. However, one cannot guarantee that edge vertices in the potential regions satisfy this requirement. Therefore, we use a modified ICP algorithm presented by Turk [64] to register the ear shape model with the edge vertices. The steps of modified ICP algorithm to register a test shape Y to a model shape X are:

1. Initialize the rotation matrix R_0 and translation vector T_0.
2. Find the closest point in X for each given point in Y.
3. Discard pairs of points which are too far apart.
4. Find the rigid transformation (R, T) such that E is minimized.
5. Apply the transformation (R, T) to Y.
6. Go to step 2 until the difference $|E_k - E_{k-1}|$ in two successive steps falls below a threshold or the maximum number of iterations is reached.

By initializing the rotation matrix R_0 and translation vector T_0 to the identity matrix and difference of centroids of two vertex sets respectively, we run ICP iteratively and finally get the rotation matrix R and translation vector T, which brings the ear shape model vertices and edge vertices into alignment. The cluster with minimum mean square error is declared as the detected ear region; the ear helix and anti-helix parts are identified in this process.

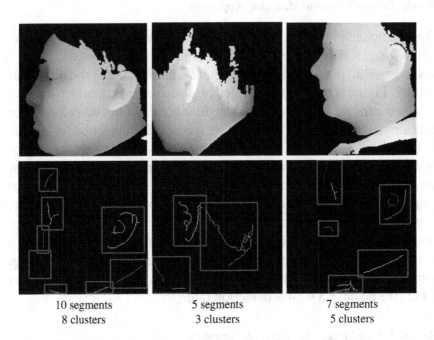

10 segments	5 segments	7 segments
8 clusters	3 clusters	5 clusters

Fig. 3.8. Examples of edge clustering results using only range images.

3.1.3 Experimental Results

Data

While we were investigating the above two approaches for 3D ear detection, we had a dataset of 52 subjects with 312 images. Each subject has at least four images. All the experimental results reported in this subsection are on the 52-subject dataset.

Results for the Template Matching Approach

We test the template matching based detection method on 312 side face range images. The parameters of the approach are $\alpha = 0.35$, $w = 5$ pixels, $\gamma = 35$ pixels and $\beta = 99$ pixels. The bin size of the histogram is 0.02. Figure 3.9 shows examples of positive detection in which the detected ears are bounded by rectangular boxes. If the detected region contains a part of an ear, we consider it a positive detection; otherwise it is a false detection. From Figure 3.9, we observe that the ear region is correctly detected. However we may obtain a part of an ear; also we may obtain parts that do not belong to an ear. Figure 3.10 shows examples of false detection. Each column in this figure shows the step edge magnitude image, the dilated binary edge map and the detection result, respectively. We have false detections since the ear helix part is not extracted. The average time to detect an ear from a side face range image is 5.2 seconds with Matlab implementation on a 2.4G Celeron CPU. We achieve a 92.4% detection rate.

Results for the Shape Model Based Approach

We test the ear shape model based detection method on 312 side face range images. If the ear shape model is aligned with the ear helix and anti-helix parts, we classify it as a positive detection; otherwise it is a false detection. In our experiments, the number of vertices in the ear shape model is 113; the average number of edge segments is 6; and the average number of clusters is 4. The average time to detect an ear from a side face range image is 6.5 seconds with Matlab implementation on a 2.4G Celeron CPU. Examples of positive detection results are shown in Figure 3.11. In Figure 3.11, the transformed ear shape model marked by yellow points is superimposed on the corresponding textured 3D face. From Figure 3.11, we can observe that the ear is

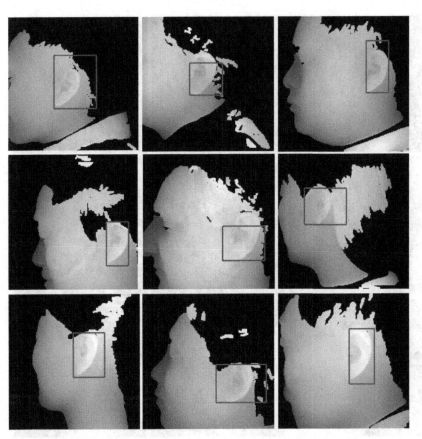

Fig. 3.9. Examples of positive detection using the template matching approach.

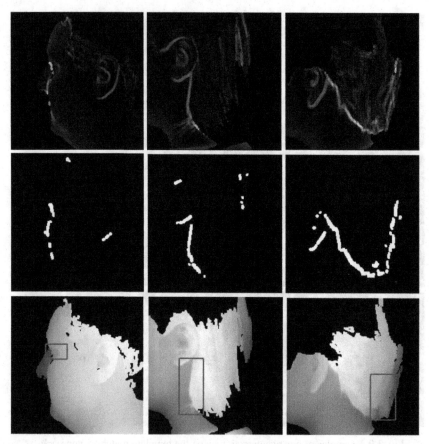

Fig. 3.10. Examples of false detection using the template matching approach. Each column shows the step edge magnitude image, the dilated binary edge map and the detection result, respectively.

correctly detected and the ear helix and anti-helix parts are identified from side face range images. The distribution of mean square error defined in equation (3.15) for the positive detection is shown in Figure 3.12. The mean of mean square error is 1.79 mm. We achieve a 92.6% detection rate.

After we locate the ear helix and anti-helix parts in a side face range image, we put a minimum rectangular bounding box that contains the detected ear. Figure 3.13 shows the examples of detected ears with a red bounding box. From Figure 3.13 and Figure 3.9, we observe that the ears in side face range images are more accurately located by the shape model-based approach. For the failed cases, we notice that there are some edge segments around the ear region caused by hair, which bring more false edge segments. This results in clusters that cannot include the ear helix and anti-helix parts. Since the ICP algorithm cannot converge due to the existence of outliers, the false detection happens; these cases are shown in Figure 3.14 and Figure 3.15. The original face range images and the corresponding edge clusters are shown in Figure 3.14. In this figure, the first row shows face images; the second row shows edge clustering results. The textured 3D faces with overlaid detected ear helix and anti-helix are shown in Figure 3.15.

3.2 3D Ear Detection Using Range and Color Images

In the above two approaches, there are some edge segments caused by non-skin pixels, which result in the false detection. Since the Minolta range sensor provides a registered 3D range image and a 2D color image, we can achieve a better detection performance by fusion of the color and range images.

The flow chart for the fusion of range and color images and global-to-local registration based detection is shown in Figure 3.16. We propose a two-step approach using the registered 2D color and range images by locating the ear helix and the anti-helix parts [1].

In the first step a skin color classifier is used to isolate the side face in an image by modeling the skin color and non-skin color distributions as a mixture of Gaussians [65]. The edges from the 2D color image are combined with the step edges from the range image to locate regions-of-interest (ROIs) that may contain an ear.

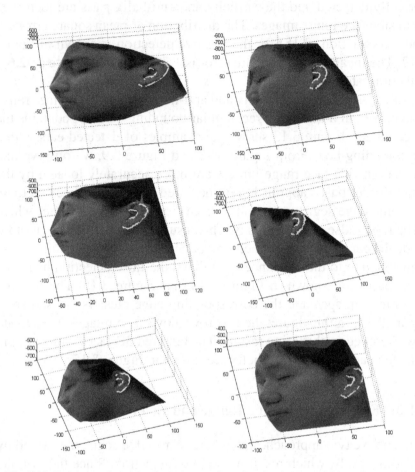

Fig. 3.11. Examples of positive detection results using the shape model based approach.

In the second step, to locate an ear accurately, the reference 3D ear shape model, which is represented by a set of discrete 3D vertices on the ear helix and the anti-helix parts, is adapted to individual ear images by following a new global-to-local registration procedure instead of training an active shape model [66] built from a large set of ears to learn the shape variation.

The DARCES (data-aligned rigidity-constrained exhaustive search) algorithm [67], which can solve the 3D rigid registration problem efficiently and reliably, without any initial estimation, is used to perform

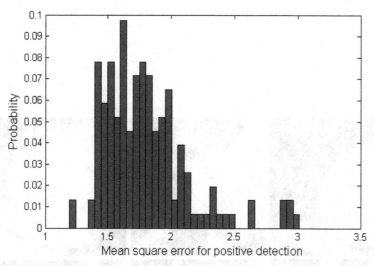

Fig. 3.12. Distribution of the mean square error for positive detection using the shape model based approach.

the global registration. This is followed by the local deformation process where it is necessary to preserve the structure of the reference ear shape model since neighboring points cannot move independently under the deformation due to physical constraints. The bending energy of thin plate spline [68], a quantitative measure for non-rigid deformations, is incorporated into the proposed optimization formulation as a regularization term to preserve the topology of the ear shape model under the shape deformation. The optimization procedure drives the initial global registration towards the ear helix and the anti-helix parts, which results in the one-to-one correspondence of the ear helix and the anti-helix between the reference ear shape model and the input image.

3.2.1 Regions-of-Interest (ROIs) Extraction

Since the images in two modalities (range and color) are registered, the ROIs can be localized in any one modality if they are known in the other modality.

• Processing of Color Images

The processing consists of two major tasks.
▶ *Skin Color Classification*: Skin color is a powerful cue for segmenting the exposed parts of the human body. Jones and Rehg [65] built a

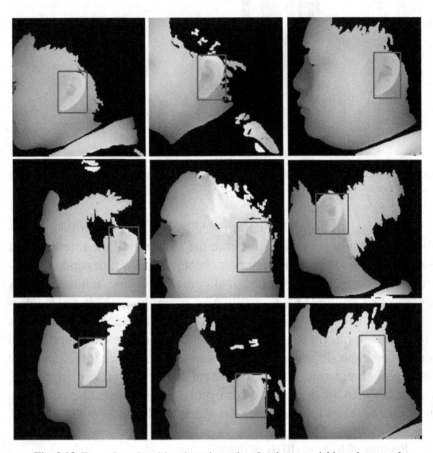

Fig. 3.13. Examples of positive detection using the shape model based approach.

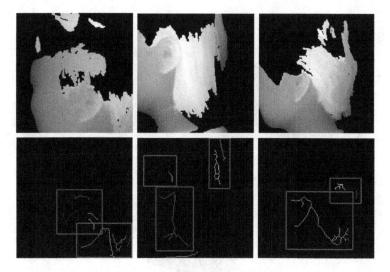

Fig. 3.14. Examples of failed cases using the shape model based approach. Each column shows the range image and the edge clustering result, respectively.

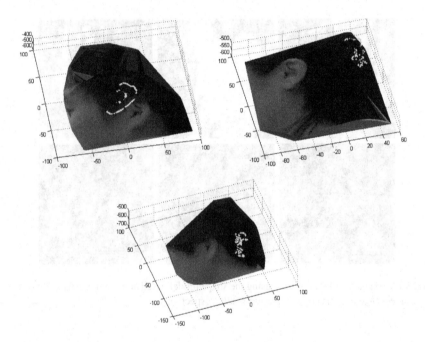

Fig. 3.15. Examples of false detection results using the shape model based approach.

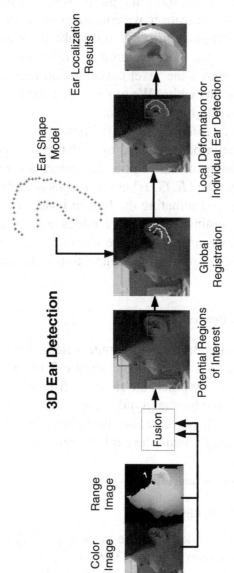

Fig. 3.16. The flow chart of ear detection by a fusion of color and range images.

classifier by learning the distributions of skin and non-skin pixels from a dataset of nearly 1 billion labeled pixels. The distributions are modeled as a mixture of Gaussians and their parameters are given in [65]. We use this method for finding skin regions. When a pixel $p(R, G, B)$ is presented for the classification, we compute *a posteriori* probability $P(\text{skin/RGB})$ and $P(\text{non-skin/RGB})$ and make the classification using the Bayesian decision theory. Figure 3.17(a) shows a color image and Figure 3.17(b) shows the pixel classification result in which the skin pixels are shown as white. We observe that the large skin region containing the ear is roughly segmented.

▶ *Edge Extraction in Intensity Images*: There are edges, around the ear helix and anti-helix parts, caused by a change in intensity. These are helpful for locating the ear region. The edges are extracted from 2D intensity images. The (R, G, B) color images are first converted to the grayscale images (eliminating the hue and saturation information while retaining the luminance) and then edges are extracted by using the Laplacian of Gaussian (LOG) edge detector (13×13 window is used). Figure 3.17(c) shows the edge detection result using the LOG detector.

● **Processing of Range Images**

As described in Section 3.1.2, we compute a step edge magnitude image for a given side face range image. Figure 3.18(a) shows a range image in which the darker pixels are far away from the camera; Figure 3.18(b) shows the step edge magnitude image in which the pixels with larger magnitudes are displayed as brighter pixels. We observe that the edge magnitude is large around the ear helix and the anti-helix parts.

Fusion of Color and Range Images

This involves the following steps.

1. The range sensor provides a range mask indicating *valid pixels* (in white), which is shown in Figure 3.19(a).
2. The range mask is combined with the skin color map to generate a final mask indicating the *valid skin pixels*, which is shown Figure 3.19(b).

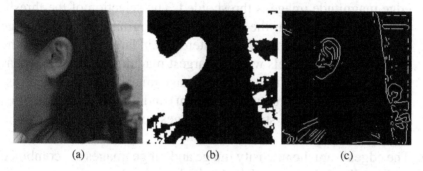

Fig. 3.17. One example of processing the color image. (a) Color image. (b) Skin color map. (c) Edge detection using a LOG edge detector.

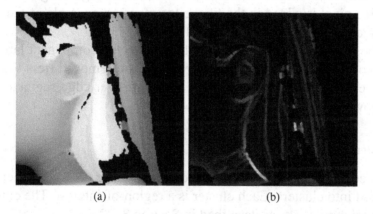

Fig. 3.18. One example of processing the range image. (a) Range image. (b) Step edge magnitude image. In image (a), the darker pixels are away from the camera and the lighter ones are closer. In image (b), the bright pixels denote large edge magnitude.

3. The final mask is applied to edge pixels from the intensity image to remove some of the pixels which are *non-skin* pixels or *invalid* pixels. "Non-skin pixels" mean the pixels that are not on the skin. "Invalid pixels" mean that the range sensor did not make measurements for these pixels. The edge pixels that are left over are shown in Figure 3.19(c).

4. For the range image, the final mask is also applied to the step edge magnitude image. In order to get edges in the range image, the step edge magnitude image is thresholded. The selection of the threshold value is based on the cumulative histogram of the step edge magnitude image. Since we are interested in larger magnitudes, the top $\eta\%$ ($\eta = 3.5$) pixels with the largest magnitudes are selected as the edge pixels. The thresholded binary image is then dilated (using a 3×3 square structuring element) and thinned (shrinking to a minimally connected stroke). The edges so obtained are shown in Figure 3.19(d).

5. The edges from the intensity image and range images are combined in the following manner. The final edge map that we expect to obtain is initialized to be the edge map of the range image (Figure 3.19(d)); for each edge pixel in the intensity image (Figure 3.19(c)) if none of its neighbors are edge pixels in the range image, then this edge pixel is added to the final edge map. An example of the final edge map is shown in Figure 3.19(e).

6. The edge pixels are labeled by the connected component labeling algorithm and the small edge segments are removed (less than 10 pixels in our experiments). The final left over edge segments are shown in Figure 3.19(f).

● **Clustering Edge Segments**

After edge segments are extracted, those close to each other are grouped into clusters. Each cluster is a region-of-interest. The clustering procedure works as described in Section 3.1.2.

Three examples of clustering results are shown in the first row of Figure 3.20, in which each cluster is bounded by a rectangular box and each edge segment is shown in different color. The second row shows the extracted regions-of-interest bounded by boxes overlaid on the color images. From Figure 3.20, we observe that the ear region is correctly identified.

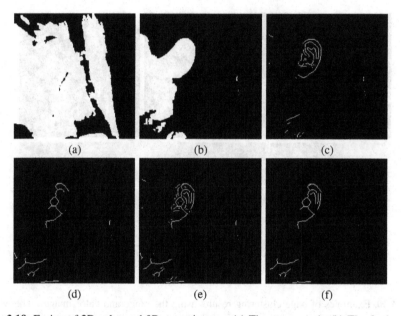

Fig. 3.19. Fusion of 2D color and 3D range images. (a) The range mask. (b) The final mask obtained by a combination of the range mask and the skin color map. (c) Edges in the intensity image after applying the final mask. (d) Edges in the range image after applying the final mask. (e) Combination of edges in both color and range images. (f) Edges after removal of small edge segments.

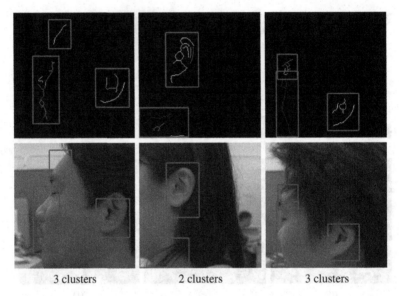

3 clusters   2 clusters   3 clusters

Fig. 3.20. Examples of edge clustering results using the range and color images. The edge segments are shown in the first row where each cluster is bounded by a rectangular box. The second rows show the ROIs superimposed on the color images.

3.2.2 Reference Ear Shape Model

Instead of training an active shape model to learn the shape variation, we adapt the reference ear shape model to input images by following a global-to-local procedure described below, in which the topology of the ear shape model is preserved during the shape deformation. We build the reference ear shape model from an instance of an ear belonging to a person which is described in Section 3.1.2.

3.2.3 Alignment of the Reference Ear Shape Model with a Region-of-Interest

Once a ROI is extracted, the ear helix and the anti-helix parts are identified by the alignment of ROI with the ear shape model. Since the rigid registration cannot account for the local shape variation between ears, we develop a global-to-local procedure: the global registration brings the reference ear shape model into coarse alignment with the ear helix and the anti-helix parts; the local deformation driven by the optimization formulation (given below) drives the reference ear shape model more close to the ear helix and the anti-helix parts.

• Global Rigid Registration

For 3D registration problem, the iterative closest point (ICP) algorithm [63] is widely used for matching points with unknown corresponding pairs. Although there are many variants of the ICP algorithm [69–71], basically it consists of two iterative steps:

1. identifying correspondences by finding the closest points;
2. computing the rigid transformation based on the corresponding pairs.

The major drawback of an ICP-based algorithm is that it needs a good initial guess of the true transformation.

The RANSAC-based data-aligned rigidity-constrained exhaustive search algorithm (DARCES) [67] can solve the registration problem without any initial estimation by using rigidity constraints to find the corresponding points. First three points (primary, secondary, and auxiliary) in the reference surface are selected; then each point on the test surface is assumed to be in correspondence to the primary point, and the other two corresponding points are found based on the rigidity constraints. For every corresponding triangle, a rigid transformation is computed and the transformation with the maximum number of over-lapping points is chosen as the solution. Due to its exhaustive nature of the search, the solution it finds is the true one.

In our case, the 3D coordinates of the reference ear shape model are known. We use the DARCES algorithm to find the corresponding triangles (between the reference ear shape model and the ROI under consideration) and the initial transformation. The ICP algorithm is then used to refine the transformation. This process is repeated for each ROI and the ROI with the minimum registration error is passed to the local deformation stage.

● **Local Deformation**

(i) **Thin Plate Spline Transformation:** The reference shape model (the ear helix and the anti-helix parts) is deformed after it is globally aligned with a ROI. Thin plate spline (TPS) transformation is a pow-erful tool for modeling the shape deformation and is widely used in shape matching [68, 72–74]. The TPS $\mathcal{R}^2 \rightarrow \mathcal{R}^2$ mapping function is defined by the following equation:

$$\mathbf{v} = f(\mathbf{u}) = \begin{bmatrix} f^x(\mathbf{u}) \\ f^y(\mathbf{u}) \end{bmatrix} = A\mathbf{u} + \mathbf{t} + \sum_{i=1}^{n} \begin{bmatrix} w_i^x \\ w_i^y \end{bmatrix} \phi(|\mathbf{u} - \mathbf{u}_i|) \quad (3.16)$$

where $\phi(r) = r^2 \log r$, $\mathbf{u} = [\hat{x}, \hat{y}]^T$, $\mathbf{v} = [x, y]^T$ and A and $\mathbf{t}$ form an affine transformation given by

$$[A \ \mathbf{t}] = \begin{bmatrix} a_{00} & a_{01} & t_0 \\ a_{10} & a_{11} & t_1 \end{bmatrix}.$$

The $n \times 2$ matrix W is given by

$$\begin{bmatrix} w_1^x & w_2^x & \cdots & w_n^x \\ w_1^y & w_2^y & \cdots & w_n^y \end{bmatrix}^T.$$

It specifies the non-linear warping where n is the number of land-mark points. Given n landmark points $\mathbf{u}(\hat{x}_i, \hat{y}_i)$ and their correspond-ing points $\mathbf{v}(x_i, y_i)$, equation (3.16) can be rewritten as $2n$ linear equations. However there are $2n+6$ unknown parameters to be solved. The following six constraints are added to make the spline function (equation (3.16)) have the square integrable second derivatives:

$$P^T[w_1^x, w_2^x, \cdots, w_n^x]^T = 0, \quad P^T[w_1^y, w_2^y, \cdots, w_n^y]^T = 0 \quad (3.17)$$

where P is a $n \times 3$ matrix defined by $(\mathbf{1}, \hat{\mathbf{x}}, \hat{\mathbf{y}})$, $\hat{\mathbf{x}} = (\hat{x}_1, \hat{x}_2, \cdots, \hat{x}_n)^T$ and $\hat{\mathbf{y}} = (\hat{y}_1, \hat{y}_2, \cdots, \hat{y}_n)^T$. The $2n + 6$ equations can be put into a compact matrix form:

$$\begin{bmatrix} \Phi & P \\ P^T & 0 \end{bmatrix} \begin{bmatrix} W \\ \mathbf{t}^T \\ A^T \end{bmatrix} = \begin{bmatrix} \mathbf{v} \\ \mathbf{0} \end{bmatrix} \qquad (3.18)$$

where the $n \times n$ matrix $\Phi_{ij} = \phi(\mathbf{u}_i - \mathbf{u}_j)$, $\mathbf{v} = (\mathbf{x}, \mathbf{y})$, $\mathbf{x} = (x_1, x_2, \cdots, x_n)^T$ and $\mathbf{y} = (y_1, y_2, \cdots, y_n)^T$. The TPS transformation minimizes the following bending energy function,

$$B_e = \iint_{\mathcal{R}^2} (F(f^x) + F(f^y))dxdy \qquad (3.19)$$

where $F(g^*(x, y)) = (g_{xx}^2 + 2g_{xy}^2 + g_{yy}^2)^*$, $*$ denotes the (x or y) under consideration and g_{xx}, g_{xy} and g_{yy} are second order derivatives. It can be shown that the value of bending energy is $B_e = \frac{1}{8\pi}(\mathbf{x}^T K\mathbf{x} + \mathbf{y}^T K\mathbf{y})$ where $\mathbf{x} = (x_1, x_2, \cdots, x_n)^T$ and $\mathbf{y} = (y_1, y_2, \cdots, y_n)^T$ [68]. The matrix K is the $n \times n$ upper left matrix of

$$\begin{bmatrix} \Phi & P \\ P^T & 0 \end{bmatrix}^{-1},$$

which only depends on the coordinates of the landmark points in $\{\mathbf{u}\}$. Therefore, the bending energy is determined by the coordinates of landmark points and their correspondences. Furthermore, the bending energy is a good measurement of the shape deformation. Since the coordinates of the reference ear shape model are known, the matrix K can be precomputed. The task is to drive the reference ear shape model towards the ROI ear such that the topology of the reference ear shape model is preserved. The bending energy is used to penalize the large shape deformation.

(ii) **Optimization Formulation:** In Section 3.2.1, we noted that there are strong step edge magnitudes in range images around the ear helix and the anti-helix parts. After we bring the reference shape model into coarse alignment with the ear helix and the anti-helix parts (in the ROI image) through the global rigid registration, we get the locations of the 3D coordinates of ear helix and anti-helix parts in the 2D color image and perform the local deformation on the 2D image plane since the 2D color image is registered with the 3D range image. In other words, we would like to drive the reference ear shape model more close to the ear helix and the anti-helix parts with the topology of the shape model preserved. We can achieve this task by minimizing the proposed new cost function:

$$E(\mathbf{x}, \mathbf{y}) = E_{img}(\mathbf{x}, \mathbf{y}) + \gamma E_D(\mathbf{x}, \mathbf{y})$$

$$= \sum_{i=1}^{n} h(|\nabla I_{\text{step}}(x_i, y_i)|)$$

$$+ \frac{1}{2}\gamma(\mathbf{x}^T K \mathbf{x} + \mathbf{y}^T K \mathbf{y}) \tag{3.20}$$

where $h(|\nabla I_{\text{step}}|) = 1/(1 + |\nabla I_{\text{step}}|)$, $|\nabla I_{\text{step}}(x_i, y_i)|$ is the step edge magnitude of ith point of the shape model located in the 2D plane and γ is a positive regularization constant that controls the topology of the shape model. For example, increasing the magnitude of γ tends to keep the topology of the ear shape model unchanged. In equation (3.20), the step edge magnitude in range images is used for the term E_{img} since edges in range images are less sensitive to the change of viewpoint and illumination than those in color images. In equation (3.20) the first term E_{img} drives points $(\mathbf{x}, \mathbf{y})$ towards the ear helix and the anti-helix parts which have larger step edge magnitudes; the second term E_D is the bending energy that preserves the topology of the reference shape model under the shape deformation. When we take the partial derivatives of equation (3.20) with respect to $\mathbf{x}$ and $\mathbf{y}$ and set them to zero, we have

$$\gamma K \mathbf{x} - \sum_{i=1}^{n} \frac{1}{(1 + |\nabla I_{\text{step}}(x_i, y_i)|)^2} \Omega^{\mathbf{x}} = 0,$$

$$\gamma K \mathbf{y} - \sum_{i=1}^{n} \frac{1}{(1 + |\nabla I_{\text{step}}(x_i, y_i)|)^2} \Omega^{\mathbf{y}} = 0. \tag{3.21}$$

In equation (3.21),

$$\Omega^{\mathbf{x}} = \frac{\partial |\nabla I_{\text{step}}(x_i, y_i)|}{\partial \mathbf{x}}$$

$$\Omega^{\mathbf{y}} = \frac{\partial |\nabla I_{\text{step}}(x_i, y_i)|}{\partial \mathbf{y}}.$$

Since K is positive semidefinite, equation (3.21) can be solved *iteratively* by introducing a step size parameter α which is shown in equation (3.22) [75]. The solutions can be obtained by matrix inversion which is shown in equation (3.23), where I is the identity matrix.

$$\gamma K \mathbf{x}_t + \alpha(\mathbf{x}_t - \mathbf{x}_{t-1}) - \mathcal{F}_{t-1}^{\mathbf{x}} = 0$$
$$\gamma K \mathbf{y}_t + \alpha(\mathbf{y}_t - \mathbf{y}_{t-1}) - \mathcal{F}_{t-1}^{\mathbf{y}} = 0 \tag{3.22}$$

In equations (3.22) and (3.23),

$$\mathcal{F}_{t-1}^{\mathbf{x}} = \sum_{i=1}^{n} \frac{1}{(1 + |\nabla I_{step}^{t-1}(x_i, y_i)|)^2} \frac{\partial |\nabla I_{step}^{t-1}(x_i, y_i)|}{\partial \mathbf{x}}$$

$$\mathcal{F}_{t-1}^{\mathbf{y}} = \sum_{i=1}^{n} \frac{1}{(1 + |\nabla I_{step}^{t-1}(x_i, y_i)|)^2} \frac{\partial |\nabla I_{step}^{t-1}(x_i, y_i)|}{\partial \mathbf{y}}.$$

$\mathcal{F}_{t-1}^{\mathbf{x}}$ and $\mathcal{F}_{t-1}^{\mathbf{y}}$ are evaluated for coordinates (x_i, y_i) at the iteration $t - 1$. $|\nabla I_{step}^{t-1}(x_i, y_i)|$ is the step edge magnitude at the location of (x_i, y_i) at the iteration $t - 1$. We have used $\alpha = 0.5$ and $\gamma = 100$ in our experiments.

$$\mathbf{x}_t = (\gamma K + \alpha I)^{-1}\left(\alpha \mathbf{x}_{t-1} + \mathcal{F}_{t-1}^{\mathbf{x}}\right)$$

$$\mathbf{y}_t = (\gamma K + \alpha I)^{-1}\left(\alpha \mathbf{y}_{t-1} + \mathcal{F}_{t-1}^{\mathbf{y}}\right) \tag{3.23}$$

3.2.4 Experimental Results

The detection experiments are performed on the UCR dataset (155 subjects with 902 shots) and the UND dataset Collection F (302 subjects with 302 pairs) and a subset of Collection G (24 subjects with 96 shots).

• Ear Detection on UCR Dataset

The proposed automatic ear detection method is tested on 902 pairs of range and color images. Figure 3.21 shows the effectiveness of the global-to-local registration procedure on three people. After the global registration, we get the positions of the 3D coordinates on the 2D image plane and their locations are marked by the bright dots which are

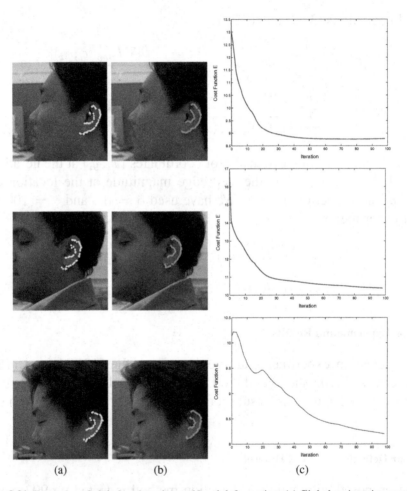

(a)   (b)   (c)

Fig. 3.21. Examples of global registration and local deformation. (a) Global registration results superimposed on the color images. (b) Local deformation results superimposed on the color images. (c) Cost function (equation (3.20)) vs. iteration.

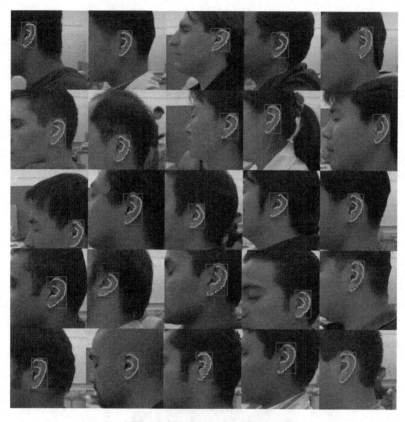

Fig. 3.22. Results of ear localization on the UCR dataset. The helix and the anti-helix parts are marked by the bright dots and the detected ear is bounded by a rectangular box.

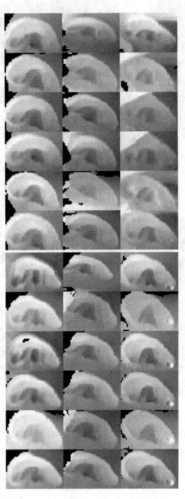

Fig. 3.23. Examples of extracted ears (from left to right and top to bottom) in the side face range images shown in Figure 1.4.

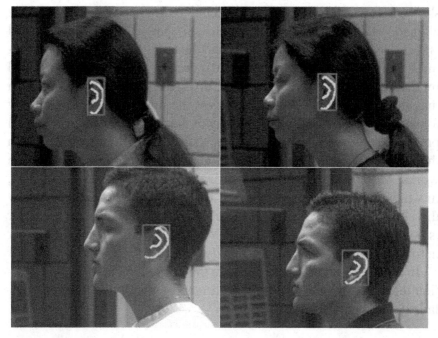

Fig. 3.24. Results of ear localization on the UND dataset shown in Figure 1.5. The helix and the anti-helix parts are marked by the bright dots and the detected ear is bounded by a rectangular box.

Table 3.2. Comparison of the three ear detection approaches.

Ear Detection Method	Detection Rate	Detection Time
Template matching	92.4% on the UCR dataset (52 subjects with 312 shots)	5.2s
Ear shape model	92.6% on the UCR dataset (52 subjects with 312 shots)	6.5s
Fusion of color/range image & global-to-local registration	99.3% on the UCR dataset (155 subjects with 902 shots), 87.71% on the UND dataset	9.48s

shown in Figure 3.21(a). It can be seen that the shape model is roughly aligned with the ear helix and the anti-helix parts. The ear shape model is then driven towards the ear helix and the anti-helix parts by minimizing the cost function (equation (3.20)) and their locations are marked by the bright dots which are shown in Figure 3.21(b). It can be seen that the optimization formulation drives the shape model more closely to the true positions with the topology of the reference ear shape model preserved. Figure 3.21(c) shows that the cost function decreases with the number of iterations, which means the optimization formulation works. More examples of ear localization are shown in Figure 3.22, in which the detected ear helix and the anti-helix parts are shown by the dots superimposed on the 2D color images and the detected ear is bounded by the rectangular box. We observe that the ears and their helix and anti-helix parts are correctly detected.

In order to quantitatively evaluate the improvement of ear localization through the local deformation driven by the optimization formulation, we compute the error

$$\varepsilon = \frac{1}{N_m} \sum_{i=1}^{N_m} \left(\frac{1}{n} \sum_{j=1}^{n} \text{Dist}(v_{ij}, G_{ti}) \right) \qquad (3.24)$$

for the global registration and the local deformation, where N_m is the number of side face range images ($N_m = 208$, since we manually labeled 3D vertices on the ear helix and the anti-helix parts for 208 images for evaluation purposes only), n is the number of points on the shape model, v_{ij} is the jth point on the shape model detected in the ith side face range image, G_{ti} is the set of manually labeled 3D points on the ear helix and the anti-helix parts of the ith side face range image and $Dist(v_{ij}, G_{ti})$ is the distance between v_{ij} and its closest point in

G_{ti}. The error ε for the global registration is 5.4mm; the error ε after the local deformation is 3.7mm. Thus, the local deformation driven by the optimization formulation really improves the localization accuracy. Figure 3.23 shows the extracted ears from the side face range images in Figure 1.4. The average number of points on the ears extracted from 902 side face images is 2,797. The ear detection takes about 9.48s with Matlab implementation on a 2.4G Celeron CPU. If the reference ear shape model is aligned with the ear helix and the anti-helix parts in a side face range image, we classify it as a positive detection; otherwise a false detection. On the 902 side face range images, we achieve 99.3% correct detection rate (896 out of 902).

● **Ear Detection on UND dataset**

Without changing the parameters of the ear detection algorithm on the UCR dataset, the proposed automatic ear detection method is tested on 700 ($302 \times 2 + 24 \times 4 = 700$) pairs of range and color images of the UND dataset (Collections F and a subset of Collection G). We achieve 87.71% correct detection rate (614 out of 700). The average number of points (on 700 images) on the ears is 6,348. Figure 3.24 shows the extracted ears from the side face range images in which the ear helix and the anti-helix are marked by bright points and the extracted ear is bounded by a rectangular box.

3.3 Conclusions

We have proposed three techniques—template matching based detection, ear shape model based detection, and fusion of color/range images and global-to-local registration based detection—to locate ears from side face range images. The comparison of the three approaches are given in Table 3.2. The first approach runs the fastest and it is simple, effective and easy to implement. The second approach locates an ear more accurately than the first approach since the shape model is used. The third approach uses both color and range images to localize the ear region accurately by following a global-to-local registration procedure. It performs the best on both the UCR and the UND datasets and it runs the slowest. Experimental results on real side face range images demonstrate the effectiveness of the proposed three approaches.

4

Recognizing 3D Ears Using Ear Helix/Anti-Helix

During the ear detection described in Chapter 3, the optimization procedure drives the initial global registration towards the ear helix and anti-helix parts, which results in the one-to-one correspondence of the ear helix and anti-helix between the reference ear shape model and the input image. We propose to match 3D ears using the ear helix/anti-helix representation [1]. First the correspondence of ear helix and anti-helix parts (available from the ear detection algorithm) between every gallery-probe ear pair is established and it is used to compute the initial rigid transformation. Then this transformation is applied to randomly selected control points of the hypothesized gallery ear in the database. A modified iterative closest point (ICP) algorithm is run to improve the transformation which brings the gallery ear and probe ear into the best alignment, for every gallery-probe pair. The root mean square (RMS) registration error is used as the matching error criterion. The subject in the gallery with the minimum RMS error is declared as the recognized person in the probe image.

4.1 Ear Helix/Anti-Helix Representation

The 3D coordinates of the ear helix and anti-helix parts are obtained from the detection algorithm and these coordinates form our ear helix/anti-helix representation. The detected ear helix/anti-helix parts are marked by the green points in Figure 4.1

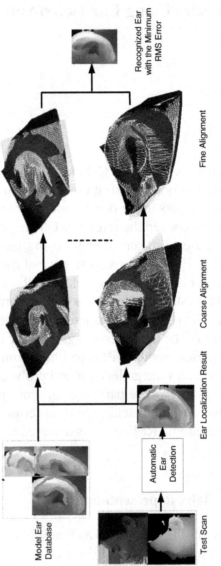

Fig. 4.1. The surface matching block diagram. The extracted ear helix and anti-helix parts are marked by the dots. The transformed model scan displayed as a mesh is overlaid on the textured test scan.

4.2 Surface Matching

As shown in the ear recognition part of Figure 4.1, the surface matching follows the coarse-to-fine strategy. Given a set of probe images, the ear and its helix and the anti-helix parts are extracted by running the detection algorithm described above. The correspondence of the helix and the anti-helix between the probe ear and the hypothesized gallery ear is used to compute the initial transformation that brings the hypothesized gallery ear into coarse alignment with the probe ear, and then a modified ICP algorithm is run to refine the transformation to bring gallery-probe pairs into the best alignment.

4.2.1 Coarse Alignment

Given two corresponding sets of N_p 3D vertices M and S on the helix and the anti-helix parts, the initial rigid transformation, which brings the gallery and the probe ears into coarse alignment, can be estimated by minimizing the sum of the squares of theses errors (equation (4.1)) with respect to the rotation matrix R and the translation vector T. The rotation matrix and translation vector are computed by using the quaternion representation [76].

$$\Sigma = \frac{1}{N_p} \sum_{l=1}^{N_p} |S_i - R * M_i - T|^2 \tag{4.1}$$

The unit quaternion is a vector $\mathbf{q_R} = [q_0, q_1, q_2, q_3]^T$, where $q_0 \geq 0$ and $q_0^2 + q_1^2 + q_2^2 + q_3^2 = 1$. The solution of R and T using the quaternion representation is performed as follows:

1. Calculate the centroid of the gallery data set M_m and the probe data set S_s given by (4.2).

$$\mu_S = \frac{1}{N_p} \sum_{i=1}^{N_p} S_i \text{ and } \mu_M = \frac{1}{N_P} \sum_{i=1}^{N_p} M_i \tag{4.2}$$

2. Calculate the covariance matrix Σ_{MS} of the sets M_m and S_s is given by

$$\Sigma_{MS} = \frac{1}{N_p} \sum_{i=1}^{N_p} [(M_i - \mu_M)(S_i - \mu_S)^T] \tag{4.3}$$

3. Construct the matrix $A_{ij} = (\Sigma_{MS} - \Sigma_{MS}^T)_{ij}$ which is used to form the column vector $\Delta = [A_{23}\ A_{31}\ A_{12}]^T$. This vector is then used to form the symmetric 4×4 matrix Q.

$$Q = \begin{bmatrix} tr(\Sigma_{MS}) & \Delta^T \\ \Delta & \Sigma_{MS} + \Sigma_{MS}^T - tr(\Sigma_{MS})I_3 \end{bmatrix} \tag{4.4}$$

where I_3 is the 3×3 identity matrix and tr is the matrix trace operator.

4. The maximum eigenvalue of Q is corresponding to the $\mathbf{q_R}$.

5. The 3×3 rotation matrix generated from a unit rotation quaternion is calculated by (4.5).

$$R = \begin{bmatrix} q_0^2 + q_1^2 - q_2^2 - q_3^2 & 2(q_1q_2 - q_0q_3) & 2(q_1q_3 + q_0q_2) \\ 2(q_1q_2 + q_0q_3) & q_0^2 + q_2^2 - q_1^2 - q_3^2 & 2(q_2q_3 - q_0q_1) \\ 2(q_1q_3 - q_0q_2) & 2(q_2q_3 + q_0q_1) & q_0^2 + q_3^2 - q_1^2 - q_2^2 \end{bmatrix}$$
$$\tag{4.5}$$

The translation vector T is calculated as $T = \mu_S - R\mu_M$.

4.2.2 Fine Alignment

Given the estimate of initial rigid transformation, the purpose of iterative closest point (ICP) algorithm [63] is to determine if the match is good and to find a refined alignment between them. If the probe ear is really an instance of the gallery ear, the ICP algorithm will result in a good registration and a large number of corresponding points between gallery and probe ear surfaces will be found. Since ICP algorithm requires that the probe be a subset of the gallery, a method to remove outliers based on the distance distribution is used [70]. The basic steps of the modified ICP algorithm are summarized below:

- Input: A 3D gallery ear range image, a 3D probe ear range image and the initial transformation obtained from the coarse alignment.
- Output: The refined transformation between the two ears.
- Procedure:
  (a) Select control points ($\sim$180) in the gallery ear range image randomly and apply the initial transformation to the gallery ear image.

(b) Find the closest points of the control points in the probe ear image and compute the statistics [70] of the distances between the corresponding pairs in the gallery and probe images.

(c) Discard some of the corresponding pairs by analyzing the statistics of the distances (a threshold is obtained based on the mean and standard deviation of distances) [70].

(d) Compute the rigid transformation between the gallery and the probe ears based on the correspondences.

(e) Apply the transformation to the gallery ear range image and repeat step b) until convergence.

Starting with the initial transformation obtained from the coarse alignment, the modified ICP algorithm is run to refine the transformation by minimizing the distance between the control points of the gallery ear and their closest points of the probe ear. For each gallery ear in the database, the control points are randomly selected and the modified ICP is applied to those points. For a selected gallery ear, we repeat the same procedure 15 times and choose the rigid transformation with the minimum root mean square (RMS) error. The subject in the gallery set with the minimum RMS error is declared as the recognized person. In the modified ICP algorithm, the speed bottleneck is the nearest neighbor search. Therefore, the K-d tree structure is used in the implementation. Figure 4.2(a) shows the coarse alignment after applying the initial rigid transformation; Figure 4.2(b) shows the refined alignment after applying the modified ICP algorithm. In Figure 4.2, the gallery ear represented by the mesh is overlaid on the textured 3D probe ear. We observe a better alignment after applying the modified ICP algorithm.

4.3 Experimental Results

In order to evaluate and compare the matching performance on the selected datasets, all the ears are correctly extracted. In these limited cases where the ears are not successfully detected in an automated manner, they are correctly extracted by human interaction.

In the UCR dataset there are 155 subjects with 902 images. The data are split into a gallery set and a probe set. Each set has 155 subjects and every subject in the probe set has an instance in the gallery set. In

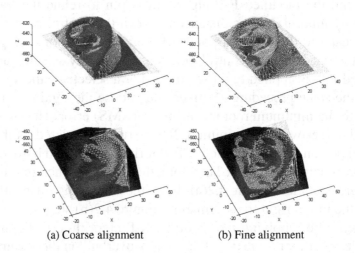

(a) Coarse alignment   (b) Fine alignment

Fig. 4.2. Two examples of coarse and fine alignment. The gallery ear represented by the mesh is overlaid on the textured 3D probe ear.

order to evaluate the proposed surface matching schemes, we perform experiments under three scenarios:

- one frontal ear of a subject is in the gallery set and another frontal ear of the same subject is in the probe set;
- two frontal ears of a subject are in the gallery set and the rest of the ear images of the same subject are in the probe set;
- two ears of a subject are randomly chosen and put in the gallery set and the rest of ear images for the same subject are in the probe set.

All the experiments are repeated five times. The three scenarios are denoted by ES_1, ES_2 and ES_3 respectively. ES_1 is used for testing the performance of the system to recognize ears with the same pose; ES_2 is used for testing the performance of the system to recognize ears with pose variations; ES_3 is used for testing the robustness of the system.

In the UND dataset Collection F, there are 302 subjects and each subject has two images. The gallery set has 302 images and the probe set has the corresponding 302 images. The experimental results on the UND dataset Collection F are obtained using the same parameters of the ear recognition algorithm as those used on the UCR dataset.

Note that the resolution of the sensors for the UCR and UND datasets are different. We anticipate improvement in performance by fine tuning the parameters on the UND dataset. However, these experiments are not performed since we wanted to keep the algorithm parameters fixed across datasets.

4.3.1 Identification Performance

Given a probe ear image, the root mean square (RMS) error is calculated for every enrolled subject in the gallery set and the subject in the gallery with the minimum RMS error is declared as the recognized person in the probe image. The matching error matrix $\{ME(i, j), i = 1, 2, \ldots, N_t, j = 1, 2, \ldots, N_m\}$ on the UCR dataset ES_1 using the helix/anti-helix representation, where N_t and N_m are the number of probe ears and gallery ears respectively, is displayed as an intensity image shown in Figure 4.3. The smaller the matching error is the more likely the two ears match. From Figure 4.3, we can see that most of the diagonal pixels are darker than the other pixels on the same row, which means correct recognition. The average time to match a pair of ears, which includes the coarse and fine alignment, is about 1.1 seconds

Table 4.1. Cumulative matching performance on the UCR dataset and the UND dataset Collection F. The number of images in the gallery and probe sets are listed in the parenthesis.

Dataset	Rank-1	Rank-2	Rank-3	Rank-4	Rank-5
$ES_1(155, 155)$	96.77%	98.06%	98.71%	98.71%	98.71%
$ES_2(310, 592)$	94.43%	96.96%	97.80%	98.31%	98.31%
	92.91%	95.95%	96.96%	97.30%	97.47%
	94.26%	95.78%	96.28%	96.45%	96.96%
$ES_3(310, 592)$	92.74%	94.76%	95.44%	95.78%	95.95%
	92.23%	95.44%	95.61%	96.45%	96.79%
	92.23%	94.93%	95.44%	95.78%	95.78%
$UND(302, 302)$	96.03%	96.69%	97.35%	97.68%	98.01%

with C++ implementation on a Linux machine with an *AMD Opteron* 1.8GHz CPU.

The identification performance is evaluated by the cumulative match characteristics (CMC), which describes "is the right answer in the top rank-r matches?". Table 4.1 shows the rank-r recognition rates for the UCR dataset and the UND dataset Collection F. In Table 4.1, the numbers of images in the gallery and the probe sets are listed in the parenthesis following the name of the dataset. We achieve 96.77% rank-1 recognition rate (150 out of 155) on the UCR dataset ES_1 and 96.03% rank-1 recognition rate (290 out of 302) on the UND dataset Collection F. As expected, the system performs better on ES_1 with the same pose and the performance degrades slightly on ES_2 with pose variations. By an inspection of the CMC values on ES_3 listed in Table 4.1, it also can be seen that the system is robust to recognize ears under different conditions. We observe that without retuning the parameters of the proposed algorithm we still achieved good recognition performance on the UND dataset which has several weeks of time lapse between the gallery and the probe.

Figure 4.4 shows three examples of the correctly recognized gallery-probe ear pairs with a large pose variation. Figure 4.4(a) shows the side face color images of the gallery and the probe alternately; Figure 4.4(b) shows the range images of the ears that are automatically extracted; Figure 4.4(c) shows the gallery ear represented by the mesh overlaid on the textured 3D probe ear images. We observe that the cases with a large pose variation are correctly handled.

We show three special cases of correctly recognizing gallery-probe ear pairs in Figures 4.5. In these two figures, the probe ear is rendered

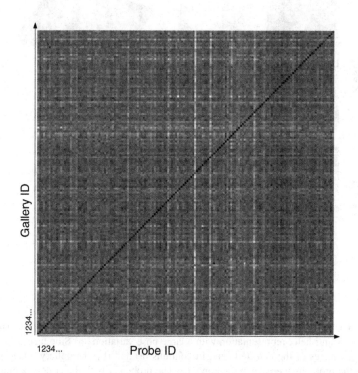

Fig. 4.3. Matching error matrix on the UCR dataset ES_1 using the ear helix/anti-helix representation displayed as an intensity image (smaller values correspond to darker pixels). The gallery ID is labeled horizontally and the probe ID is labeled vertically.

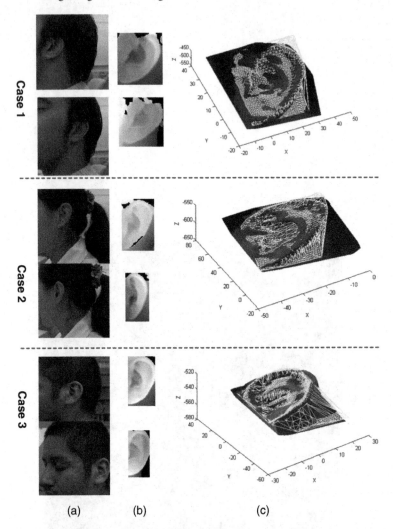

Fig. 4.4. UCR dataset: Three cases of the correctly recognized gallery-probe ear pairs using the ear helix/anti-helix representation with a large pose variation. (a) Side face color images. (b) Range images of the detected ears. In columns (a) and (b), the gallery image is shown first and the probe image is shown second. (c) The probe ear with the corresponding gallery ear after alignment. The gallery ear represented by the mesh is overlaid on the textured 3D probe ear. The units of x, y and z are millimeters (mm). In case 1, the rotation angle is $33.5°$ and the axis is $[0.0099, \ 0.9969, \ 0.0778]^T$. In case 2, the rotation angle is $-33.5°$ and the axis is $[-0.1162, 0.9932, 0.0044]^T$. In case 3, the rotation angle is $32.9°$ and the axis is $[0.0002, \ 0.9998, \ 0.0197]^T$.

as a textured 3D surface; the gallery ear is displayed as a mesh. In order to examine our results visually, we display the gallery ear and probe ear in the same image (Figure 4.5(b)) and also the transformed gallery and probe ear in the same image (Figure 4.5(c)). From Figure 4.5, we observe that the ear recognition system can handle partial occlusion. Twelve more examples of correctly recognized gallery-probe ear pairs are shown in Figure 4.6. The images in the columns (a) and (c) display test ears and their corresponding gallery ears before alignment; the images in the columns (b) and (d) show probe ears and correctly recognized gallery ears after alignment. From Figure 4.6, we see that each gallery ear is well aligned with the corresponding probe ear.

During the recognition, some errors are made and four cases are illustrated in Figure 4.7. Figure 4.7(a) and (b) show the color images of two visually similar probe and gallery ears that belong to different subjects; Figure 4.7(c) shows the true gallery ear overlaid on the textured 3D probe ear after registration; Figure 4.7(d) shows the falsely recognized gallery ear overlaid on the textured 3D probe ear after alignment. In Figure 4.7(d), the root mean square error for the falsely recognized ear is smaller than the error for the correct ear in Figure 4.7(c). Since we pick up the gallery ear with the minimum RMS error as the recognized ear, we made the errors. In this figure, we obtain good alignment between the gallery and model ears from different persons since these ears are quite similar in 3D.

4.3.2 Verification Performance

The verification performance of the proposed system is evaluated in terms of the two popular methods, the receiver operating characteristic (ROC) curve and the equal error rate (EER). The ROC curve is the plot of genuine acceptance rate (GAR) versus the corresponding false acceptance rate (FAR). GAR is defined as the percentage of the occurrences that an authorized user is correctly accepted by the system, while FAR is defined as the percentage of the occurrences that a non-authorized user is falsely accepted by the system. The EER, which indicates the rate at which false rejection rate ($FRR = 1 - GAR$) and the false acceptance rate are equal, is a threshold independent performance measure.

During the verification, the RMS distance is computed from matching the gallery ears to the probe ears and it is then compared to a

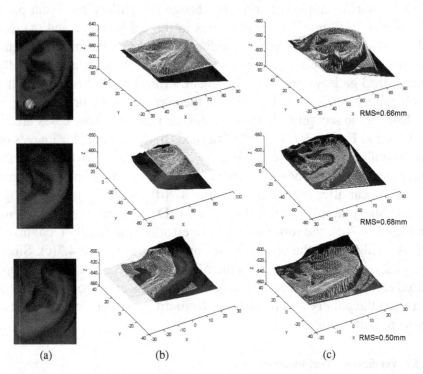

(a)   (b)   (c)

Fig. 4.5. Three special cases of correctly recognized gallery-probe ears using the ear helix/anti-helix representation, in which ears are partially occluded by an earring or by the hair. (a) Color images of the ears. (b) Examples of probe ears with the corresponding gallery ears before alignment. (c) Examples of test ears with the correctly recognized gallery ears after alignment. The gallery ear represented by the mesh is overlaid on the textured 3D test ear. The units of x, y and z are millimeters (mm).

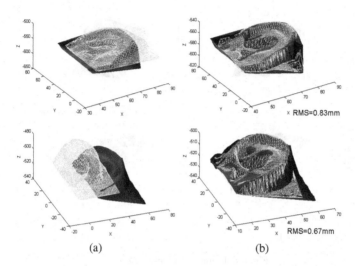

(a)   (b)

Fig. 4.6. UCR dataset: Twelve cases of the correctly recognized gallery-probe pairs using the ear helix/anti-helix representation. (a) Examples of probe ears with the corresponding gallery ears before alignment. (b) Examples of probe ears with the correctly recognized gallery ears after alignment. The gallery ear represented by the mesh is overlaid on the textured 3D probe ear. The units of x, y and z are millimeters (mm).

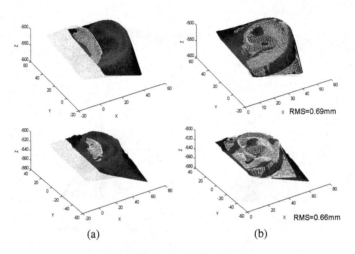

(a)   (b)

Fig. 4.6. Figure 4.6 Continued.

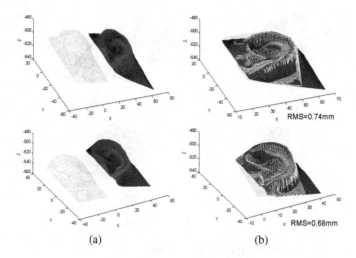

(a)   (b)

Fig. 4.6. Figure 4.6 Continued.

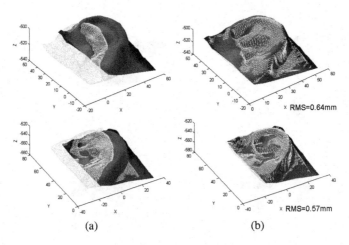

(a)   (b)

Fig. 4.6. Figure 4.6 Continued.

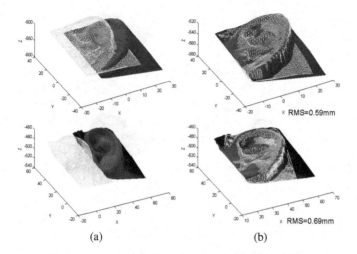

(a)   (b)

Fig. 4.6. Figure 4.6 Continued.

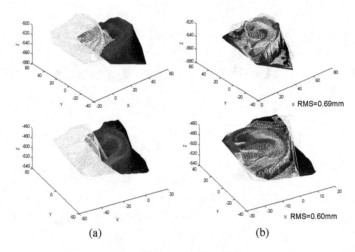

(a)   (b)

Fig. 4.6. Figure 4.6 Continued.

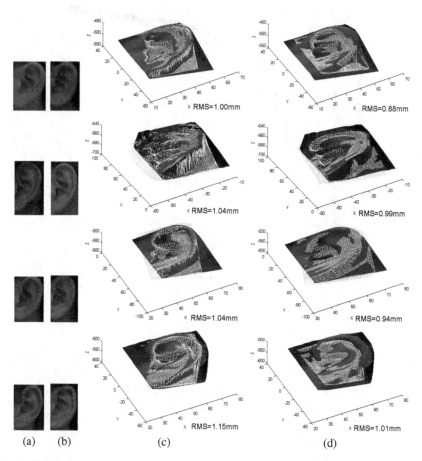

(a)   (b)   (c)   (d)

Fig. 4.7. UCR dataset: Four cases of incorrectly recognized gallery-probe pairs using the ear helix/anti-helix. Each row shows one case. The gallery ears represented by the mesh are overlaid on the textured 3D probe ears. The units of x, y and z are millimeters (mm). (a) Color images of the probe ears. (b) Color images of falsely recognized gallery ears. (c) True gallery ears after alignment are overlaid on the textured 3D probe ears. (d) The falsely recognized gallery ears after alignment are overlaid on the textured 3D probe ears. Note that for the incorrect matches the gallery ears in column (d) achieve a smaller value of RMS error than the gallery ears in column (c).

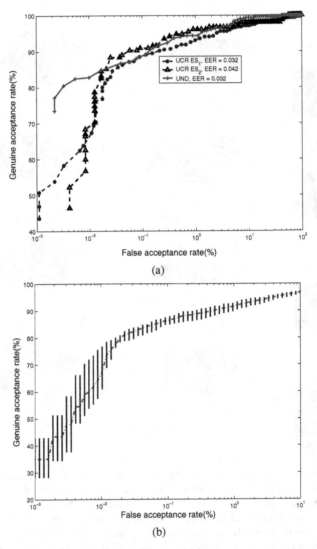

Fig. 4.8. UCR dataset and UND dataset Collection F: Verification performance as a ROC curve using the ear helix/anti-helix representation. (a) ROC curves on the UCR dataset ES_1, ES_2 and the UND dataset. (b) ROC curve on the UCR dataset ES_3. The dotted line is the average of GAR over a particular FAR and the vertical line indicates the range of GAR for a particular FAR over 5 runs. The EERs for the 5 runs are 0.042, 0.043, 0.049, 0.045, and 0.055, respectively.

threshold to determine if the probe is an authorized user or an imposter. By varying the threshold FAR and GAR values are computed and plotted in Figure 4.8. Figure 4.8(a) shows the ROC curves on the UCR dataset ES_1, ES_2 and the UND dataset; Figure 4.8(b) shows the ROC curve on the UCR dataset ES_3. As expected, the system performs best on ES_1 with a 0.032 EER. It can be seen that EERs changed slightly on the three scenarios, which suggests that the system is capable of verifying ears with pose variations and partial occlusions.

4.4 Conclusions

We have proposed the ear helix/anti-helix representation for surface matching in 3D. The 3D coordinates of the ear helix/anti-helix parts are obtained from the detection algorithm and they are used to estimate the initial transformation between a gallery-probe pair. Then a modified ICP algorithm iteratively refines the transformation which brings the hypothesized gallery and a probe into the best alignment. We have performed extensive experiments the UCR dataset (155 subject with 902 images) and the UND dataset Collection F (302 subject with 302 time-lapse pairs). It is encouraging to observe that the proposed ear recognition system is capable of recognizing ears with pose variation and partial occlusions.

5

Recognizing 3D Ears Using Local Surface Patches

In this chapter, we use the local surface patch (LSP) representation for matching 3D ears [1, 12]. The LSP representation, a new local surface descriptor, is characterized by a centroid, a local surface type and a 2D histogram. The 2D histogram shows the frequency of occurrence of shape index values vs. the angles between the normal of reference feature point and that of its neighbors. The proposed human recognition system using the LSP representation is illustrated in Figure 5.1. The local surface descriptors are computed for the feature points which are defined as either the local minimum or the local maximum of shape indexes. By comparing the local surface patches for a gallery and a probe image, the potential corresponding local surface patches are established and then filtered by geometric constraints. Based on the filtered correspondences, the initial rigid transformation is estimated. Once this transformation is obtained, it is then applied to randomly selected control points of the hypothesized gallery ear in the database. A modified iterative closest point (ICP) algorithm is run to improve the transformation which brings a gallery ear and a probe ear into the best alignment, for every gallery-probe pair. The root mean square (RMS) registration error is used as the matching error criterion. The subject in the gallery with the minimum RMS error is declared as the recognized person in the probe image.

5.1 Local Surface Patch Representation (LSP)

In 3D object recognition, the key problems are how to represent free-form surfaces effectively and how to match the surfaces using the

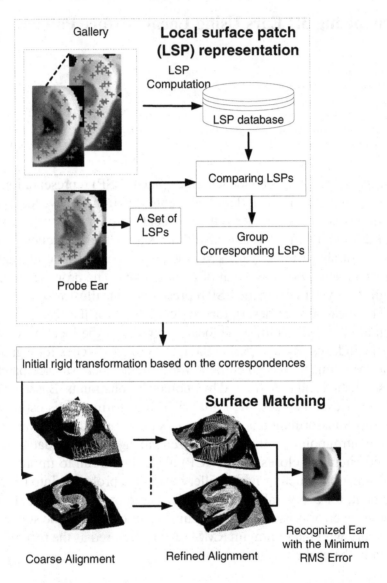

Fig. 5.1. The 3D ear recognition using the local surface patch (LSP) representation.

selected representation. Researchers have proposed various surface signatures for recognizing 3D free-form objects which are reviewed in [12, 51]. In the following, we present a new surface representation, called the local surface patch (LSP), investigate its properties and use it for ear recognition.

5.1.1 Definition of LSP

We define a "local surface patch" (LSP) as the region consisting of a feature point P and its neighbors N. The LSP representation includes feature point P, its surface type, centroid of the patch, and a histogram of shape index values vs. dot product of the surface normal at point P and its neighbors. A local surface patch is shown in Figure 5.2. The neighbors satisfy the following conditions,

$$N = \{\text{pixels} \quad N, ||N - P|| \le \epsilon_1\}$$
$$\text{and } \text{acos}(n_p \bullet n_n < A), \tag{5.1}$$

where $\bullet$ denotes the dot product between the surface normal vectors n_p and n_n at point P and N and acos denotes the inverse cosine function. The two parameters ϵ_1 and A ($\epsilon_1 = 5.8$mm, $A = 0.5$) are important since they determine the descriptiveness of the local surface patch representation. A local surface patch is not computed at every pixel in a range image, but only at selected feature points.

The feature points are defined as the local minimum and the maximum of shape indexes, which can be calculated from principal curvatures. The curvatures can be estimated as described in Section 3.1.1.

Shape index (S_i), a quantitative measure of the shape of a surface at a point P, is defined by equation (5.2),

$$S_i(P) = \frac{1}{2} - \frac{1}{\pi} \tan^{-1} \frac{k_1(P) + k_2(P)}{k_1(P) - k_2(P)} \tag{5.2}$$

where k_1 and k_2 are maximum and minimum principal curvatures, respectively. With this definition, all shapes are mapped into the interval [0, 1] [77]. The shape categories and corresponding shape index ranges are listed in Table 3.1. Figure 5.3 shows original ear range images and their shape index images for two people. In this figure, the brighter pixels denote large shape index values which correspond to ridge and

Table 5.1. Surface type Tp based on the value of shape index.

Type tag (Tp)	S_i range	Surface type
0	[0,5/16)	Concave
1	[5/16,11/16)	Saddle
2	[11/16,1]	Convex

dome surfaces while the darker pixels denote small shape index values that correspond to valley and cup surfaces. Within a $b \times b$ ($b = 5$) window, the center point is marked as a feature point if its shape index is higher or lower than those of its neighbors. The results of feature points extraction are shown in Figure 5.4 where the feature points are marked by red plus sign. In order to see the feature points' location, we enlarge the two images. We can clearly see that some feature points corresponding to the same physical area appear in both images.

For every local surface patch, we compute the shape indexes and normal angles between point P and its neighbors. Then we form a 2D histogram by accumulating points in particular bins along the two axes. One axis of this histogram is the shape index which is in the range [0,1]; the other is the dot product of surface normal vectors at P and N which is in the range $[-1, 1]$. In order to reduce the effect of noise, we use bilinear interpolation when we calculate the 2D histogram. One example of 2D histogram is shown as a grayscale image in Figure 5.2(c); the brighter areas in the image correspond to bins with more points falling into them. In the implementation, the number of bins for the shape index axis is 17 and the number of bins for the other axis is 34.

We classify surface shape of a local surface patch into three types: concave (Tp = 0), saddle (Tp = 1) and convex (Tp = 2) based on the shape index value of the feature point. The shape index range and its corresponding surface type are listed in Table 5.1. We also compute the centroid of a local surface patch. Note that a feature point and the centroid of a patch may not coincide.

In summary, every local surface patch is described by a 2D histogram, surface type, and the centroid. The 2D histogram and surface type are used for comparison of LSPs and the centroid is used for computing the rigid transformation. The patch encodes the geometric information of a local surface.

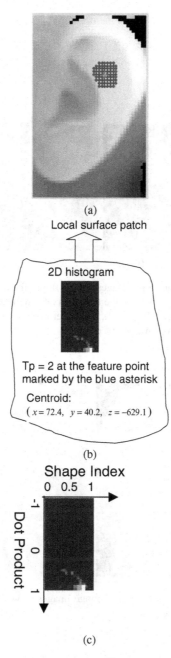

(a)
Local surface patch

2D histogram

Tp = 2 at the feature point
marked by the blue asterisk

Centroid:
$(x = 72.4, \quad y = 40.2, \quad z = -629.1)$

(b)

Shape Index
0 0.5 1

Dot Product
-1 0 1

(c)

Fig. 5.2. Illustration of a local surface patch (LSP). (a) Feature point P is marked by the asterisk and its neighbors N are marked by the interconnected dots. (b) LSP representation includes a 2D histogram, a surface type and centroid coordinates. (c) The 2D histogram is shown as a gray image in which the brighter areas correspond to bins with the high frequency of occurrence.

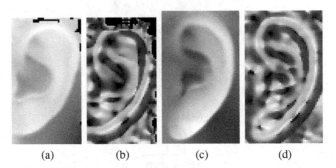

(a)   (b)   (c)   (d)

Fig. 5.3. Two examples of ear range images ((a), (c)) and their corresponding shape index images ((b), (d)). In images (a) and (c), the darker pixels are away from the camera and the lighter ones are closer. In images (b) and (d), the darker pixels correspond to concave surfaces and lighter ones correspond to convex surfaces.

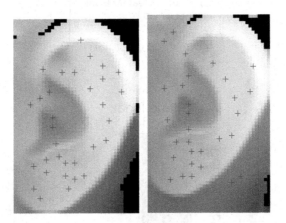

Fig. 5.4. Feature points location (+) in two range images shown as grayscale images of the same ear taken at different viewpoints.

5.1.2 Comparing Local Surface Patches

Given a probe range image, we extract feature points and get local surface patches. Considering the inaccuracy of feature points' location, we also extract local surface patches from the neighbors of feature points. Then we compare them with all of the local surface patches saved in the gallery based on the surface type and histogram dissimilarity. We use a statistical method to assess the dissimilarity between the two probability density functions since a histogram can be thought of as an unnormalized approximation to it. The $\chi^2 - divergence$ is among the most prominent divergence used in statistics to assess the dissimilarity between two probability density functions. We use it to measure the dissimilarity between two observed histograms Q and V, as follows [62]:

$$\chi^2(Q,V) = \sum_i \frac{(q_i - v_i)^2}{q_i + v_i} \tag{5.3}$$

From equation (5.3), we know the dissimilarity is between 0 and 2. If the two histograms are exactly the same, the dissimilarity will be zero. If the two histograms do not overlap with each other, it will achieve the maximum value of 2.

Figure 5.5 shows an experimental validation that the local surface patch has the discriminative power to distinguish shapes. We do experiments under three cases:

- A local surface patch (LSP1) generated for an ear is compared to another local surface patch (LSP2) corresponding to the same physical area of the same ear imaged from a different viewpoint; in this case a low dissimilarity exists and both LSPs have the same surface type.
- The LSP1 is compared to LSP3 which lies in a different area of the same ear; the dissimilarity is high and they have different surface type.
- The LSP1 is compared to LSP4 which lies in the similar area as the LSP1 but it is not the same ear; there exists a higher dissimilarity than the first case and they also have the different surface type.

These experimental results suggest that the local surface patch provides distinguishable features and it can be used for differentiation among ears. Table 5.2 shows the comparison results.

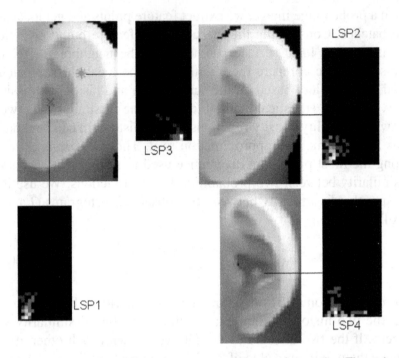

Fig. 5.5. The demonstration of discriminatory power of local surface patches. The ear images in the first row are from the same person but with different viewpoints. The ear image shown in the second row is from a different person. The histograms of four local surface patches (LSP1 to LSP4) are also shown for the comparison.

Table 5.2. Comparison results for four local surface patches shown in Figure 5.5.

Surface Type	LSP1	LSP2	LSP3	LSP4
	Tp=0	Tp=0	Tp=2	Tp=1
χ^2 − divergence	$\chi^2(LSP1, LSP2)$	$\chi^2(LSP1, LSP3)$	$\chi^2(LSP1, LSP4)$	
	0.479	1.99	0.984	

5.1.3 Generating Parameters of LSP

There are four parameters that control the generation of an LSP: the number of bins for the shape index, the number of bins for the dot product of surface normal vectors, the distance constraint ϵ_1, and the angle constraint A. Figure 5.6 and 5.7 show quantitative analysis of the effect of these four parameters. We compute χ^2 dissimilarity for corresponding and non-corresponding LSPs versus different generating parameters. Since the gallery/probe pair is registered, we can easily determine correspondence in the probe range image for every extracted feature point in the gallery range image. If we only consider the dissimilarity between corresponding LSPs, it is not sufficient to analyze the effect of generating parameters on comparing LSPs. We need to take into account the dissimilarity for both corresponding LSPs and non-corresponding LSPs to analyze the effect of generating parameters. In order to get non-corresponding points, we move their correspondences in the probe image to other locations to make them at least 15mm apart (the average length of ear is about 62mm). For every corresponding LSP, we compute the dissimilarity for corresponding LSPs and get the mean. By repeating the same procedure for different generating parameters, we create the plot of χ^2 dissimilarity for corresponding LSPs versus the varying parameter. We repeat the same procedure for non-corresponding LSPs and obtain the plot of χ^2 dissimilarity versus the varying parameter. We analyze the effect of each parameter while keeping other three fixed.

In Figure 5.6 and 5.7 there are three curves: two of them are plots of the mean of dissimilarity versus the varying parameter; the other one is the plot of the separability versus the varying parameter. Assuming the distributions for corresponding and non-corresponding LSPs are Gaussian, the separability is defined by $\frac{|\mu_1 - \mu_2|}{\sqrt{(\sigma_1^2 + \sigma_2^2)}}$, where μ_1, σ_1 and μ_2, σ_2 are the mean and standard deviation of dissimilarity for corresponding and non-corresponding LSPs respectively. The separability measures the distance between the dissimilarity distribution for corresponding and non-corresponding LSPs to some degree.

The *number of bins* is an important parameter since it controls the size of 2D histogram and it also affects the descriptiveness of LSPs. If the number of bins is small, the possibility of points falling into the same bin is large, and the χ^2 dissimilarity for corresponding and non-corresponding LSPs will be small. As the number of bins increases, the χ^2 dissimilarity for corresponding and non-corresponding LSPs increases since the chances of points falling into different bins are higher, which results in the decrease in the overlap of histograms corresponding to two LSPs. Figure 5.6(a), (b) and 5.7(a), (b) verify the analysis. We can also observe that the separability increases with the increasing number of bins and then decreases, which confirms the intuition that too few bins and too many bins are not good choices for generating surface signatures.

The *distance constraint* controls the number of points contributing to the generation of a LSP. Larger distance constraint allows for more points to be included in a LSP. Intuitively the larger distance constraint results in more discriminating LSPs since LSPs encode more surface information. The intuition is confirmed by the curve of dissimilarity versus the distance constraint in Figure 5.6(c) and 5.7(c), which show that the dissimilarity drops with the increase in distance constraint. It may seem that we should set the distance constraint as large as possible. However, the dissimilarity for non-corresponding LSPs also drops with the distance constraint increasing. From Figure 5.6(c) and 5.7(c), we also observe that the separability increases then drops when the distance constraint increases, which suggests that there is a tradeoff between the descriptiveness of a LSP and the distance constraint.

The *angle constraint* controls the effect of self occlusion. The small value of angle constraint allows for a small number of points contributing to the generation of a LSP, resulting in the large dissimilarity. As the angle constraint is relaxed, the number of points included as a part of a LSP increases. Therefore, in this case an LSP encodes more shape information and the dissimilarity should decrease. As the angle constraint becomes more relaxed the dissimilarity may increase since the shape becomes more and more unique. Figure 5.6(d) and Figure 5.7(d) show that initially dissimilarity decreases and then increases slowly as the angle constraint increases. The separability increases as the angle constraint increases. It seems that we should set the angle constraint as large as possible. However, a small angle constraint is necessary for limiting the effect of occlusion.

The surface type, another component of LSP representation, only depends on the reference point of LSP, and is not affected by the four generating parameters.

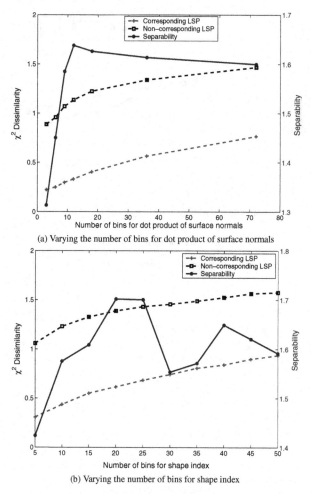

(a) Varying the number of bins for dot product of surface normals

(b) Varying the number of bins for shape index

Fig. 5.6. Effect of generating parameters of LSP on comparing LSPs obtained from one gallery/probe pair ((a)-(d)).

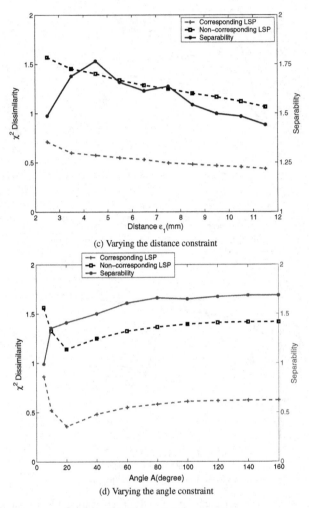

(c) Varying the distance constraint

(d) Varying the angle constraint

Fig. 5.6. Figure 5.6 Continued.

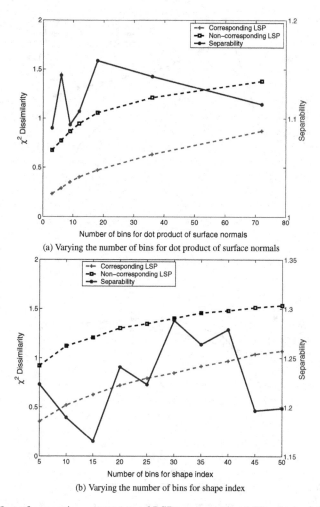

(a) Varying the number of bins for dot product of surface normals

(b) Varying the number of bins for shape index

Fig. 5.7. Effect of generating parameters of LSP on comparing LSPs obtained from another gallery/probe pair ((a)-(d)).

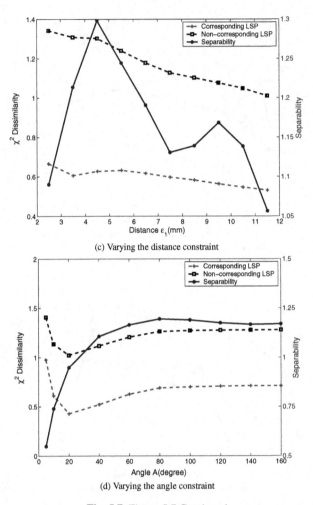

(c) Varying the distance constraint

(d) Varying the angle constraint

Fig. 5.7. Figure 5.7 Continued.

5.1.4 Invariance of Local Surface Patches to Rigid Transformation

The LSP representation consists of histogram of shape index and surface normal angle which are invariant to rigid transformation. To verify this, we compute the χ^2 dissimilarity between reference LSPs and
their corresponding LSPs after rigid transformation. We synthetically
generate range images at different views by applying 3D rigid transformation. Given a range image $\{v = \{x, y, z\}\}$, we apply the transformation $(tv = R(v - v_0) + v_0)$ to generate new views where v_0 is
the centroid of 3D vertices in the original range image, R is the rotation matrix and tv are new 3D coordinates after transformation. The
rotation matrix R can be written as $R = R_\phi * R_\beta * R_\alpha$ where R_ϕ, R_β,
R_α are rotation matrices along x-axis, y-axis, and z-axis, respectively.
We calculate shape index and surface normals for the synthetic range
image, compute LSPs at the same location as the reference LSPs, and
compute the χ^2 dissimilarity between the two corresponding LSPs for
the extracted feature points. The surface type for the corresponding
LSP is not changed by the rigid transformation. The dissimilarity distributions are shown in Figure 5.8.

Figure 5.8(a) and (b) show the distributions for two different rota-
tions. From this figure, we observe the dissimilarity does not change
much and LSP representation is invariant to rigid transformation. Furthermore, as described in Section 5.3, we performed experiments on
the UCR dataset which has pose variations ($\pm 35°$) for six different
shots of the same subject and on a subset of the UND dataset Collection G which has pose variations (up to $45°$) for four shots of the
same subject. We achieved good performance. These results show the
robustness and view-point invariance of the LSP representation.

5.1.5 Robustness of Local Surface Patches in the Presence of Noise

In order to use the proposed LSP representation for recognizing 3D
objects from real data, we need to address the problem of robustness
of LSP in the presence of noise. Since LSP is a local surface descriptor, it will be robust to certain levels of noise. We verify this hypothesis experimentally. While the noise model for different range sensors
may be different, we use the Gaussian noise model for the Minolta
Vivid camera [78]. Other examples of additive Gaussian noise model
with the range data can be found in [79, 80]. Therefore, we inject zero

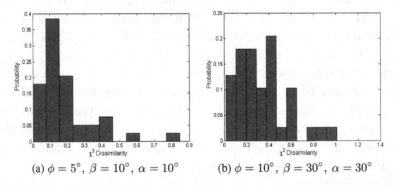

(a) $\phi = 5°$, $\beta = 10°$, $\alpha = 10°$ (b) $\phi = 10°$, $\beta = 30°$, $\alpha = 30°$

Fig. 5.8. χ^2 dissimilarity for corresponding LSPs with respect to the rigid transformation.

(a)   (b)   (c)

Fig. 5.9. Visualization of a surface corrupted by Gaussian noise $N(\mu, \sigma)$. (a) No noise added. (b) $N(\mu = 0, \sigma = 0.6mm)$. (c) $N(\mu = 0, \sigma = 1.0mm)$.

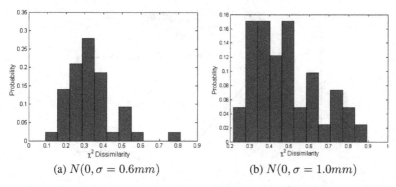

(a) $N(0, \sigma = 0.6mm)$ (b) $N(0, \sigma = 1.0mm)$

Fig. 5.10. χ^2 dissimilarity for corresponding LSPs in the presence of noise.

mean Gaussian noise $N(0, \sigma^2)$ to range images along the viewing direction (Z-axis). The standard deviation of Gaussian noise that we add depends on the mesh resolution of range scans. However the mesh resolution is not well defined. We use the Johnson's definition [3] according to which "Mesh resolution is defined as the median of all edge lengths in a mesh." Given a range image, we triangulate it and get a triangular mesh. Then we calculate the median of all edge lengths in the mesh. The average median calculated from range scans is about 1.25mm. Adding noise to range images will corrupt the surface and examples of a range image corrupted with Gaussian noise are shown in Figure 5.9.

Given a range image, we add zero mean Gaussian noise with $\sigma = 0.6$mm and $\sigma = 1.0$mm, then we compute the LSP at the same location as the reference LSP on the corrupted range image, next we calculate the χ^2 dissimilarity between corresponding LSPs. Figure 5.10 shows the distribution of dissimilarity with added Gaussian noise. From Figure 5.10, we can see that the LSP representation is robust to Gaussian noise with $\sigma = 0.6$mm and performs a little worse to Gaussian noise with $\sigma = 1.0$mm. Since the noise corrupts the surface, 14% of corresponding LSPs change the surface type. The dissimilarity for corresponding and non-corresponding LSPs and the separability versus the increased corruption for two different ears are shown in Figure 5.11. We can observe that the dissimilarity for corresponding LSPs increases slowly since the noise corrupts the surface shape and the separability decreases with the increase in corruption, which suggests that LSP matching degrades slowly as the noise level increases.

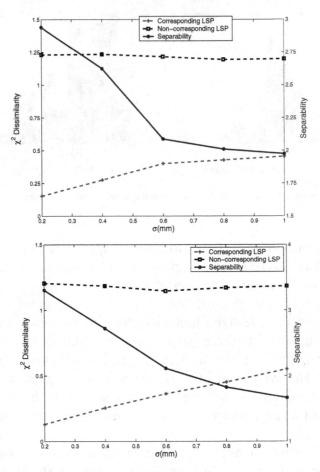

Fig. 5.11. χ^2 dissimilarity for corresponding LSPs with respect to noise of different σ.

5.1.6 Comparison with Spin Image Representation

It is to be noted that our LSP representation is different from the spin image representation [3]. Unlike the LSP representation, spin image is a 2D histogram described by two parameters: distance to the tangent plane of the oriented point from its neighbors and the distance to the normal vector of the oriented point. As described above, we compute LSPs for feature points, while the spin image is computed for every vertex on the surface of an object [3]. In Section 5.3.4, we provide a comparison of the LSP and the spin image representations on a ear dataset.

5.2 Surface Matching

5.2.1 Grouping Corresponding Pairs of LSPs

Given a probe range image, we extract feature points and get local surface patches. Considering the inaccuracy of feature points' location, we also extract local surface patches from neighbors of feature points. Then we compare them with all of the local surface patches saved in the model database. This comparison is based on the surface type and χ^2 dissimilarity mentioned in Section 5.1.2.

For every local surface patch from the probe ear, we choose the local surface patch from the database with minimum dissimilarity and the same surface type as the possible corresponding patch. We filter the possible corresponding pairs based on the geometric constraints given below.

$$d_{C_1,C_2} = |d_{S_1,S_2} - d_{M_1,M_2}| < \epsilon_2$$
$$\max(d_{S_1,S_2}, d_{M_1,M_2}) > \epsilon_3 \qquad (5.4)$$

where d_{S_1,S_2} and d_{M_1,M_2} are Euclidean distances between centroids of two surface patches. The first constraint guarantees that distances d_{S_1,S_2} and d_{M_1,M_2} are consistent; the second constraint removes the correspondences which are too close. For two correspondences $C_1 = \{S_1, M_1\}$ and $C_2 = \{S_2, M_2\}$ where S_i is probe surface patch and M_i is gallery surface patch, they should satisfy (5.4) if they are consistent corresponding pairs. Therefore, we use simple geometric constraints to partition the potential corresponding pairs into different groups. The larger the group is, the more likely it contains the true corresponding pairs.

Given a list of corresponding pairs $L = \{C_1, C_2, \ldots, C_n\}$, the grouping procedure for every pair in the list is as follows:

- Initialize each pair of a group.
- For every group, add other pairs to it if they satisfy (5.4).
- Repeat the same procedure for every group.
- Sort the groups in the ascending order based on the size of groups.
- Select the groups on the top of the list.

Figures 5.12 and 5.13 show two examples of partitioning corresponding pairs into different groups. Figure 5.12 shows a pair of ears with a small pose variation and Figure 5.13 shows a pair of ears with a large pose variation. Figures 5.12 and 5.13(a) show the feature point extraction results for the probe ears. Comparing the local surface patches with LSPs on the gallery ear, the initial corresponding pairs are shown in Figure 5.12 and 5.13(b), in which every pair is represented by the same number superimposed on the probe and gallery images. We observe that both the true and false corresponding pairs are found. Applying the simple geometric constraints (5.4), examples of filtered groups are shown in Figures 5.12 and 5.13(c) (d), respectively. We can see that the true corresponding pairs are obtained by comparing local surface patches and using the simple geometric constraints for ear pairs with small or large pose variations.

5.2.2 Alignment of Gallery with Probe Ears

Once the corresponding LSPs between the gallery and probe are established, the initial rigid transformation is estimated and the coarse-to-fine surface matching strategy is followed (see Section 4.2).

5.3 Experimental Results

As described in Section 4.3 about the dataset, we perform experiments on the UCR dataset ES_1 and ES_2 and on the UND dataset Collection F and a subset of Collection G (24 subjects with four orientations). The experimental results on the UND dataset Collection F and G are obtained by using the *same* parameters of the ear recognition algorithm as those used on the UCR dataset.

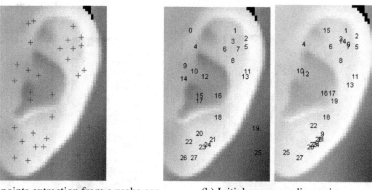

(a) Feature points extraction from a probe ear   (b) Initial corresponding pairs

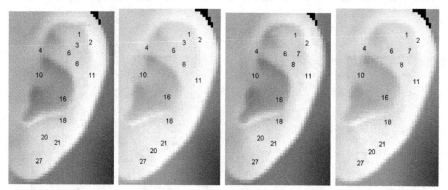

(c) Example of filtered corresponding pairs   (d) Example of filtered corresponding pairs

Fig. 5.12. Example of grouping corresponding LSPs for a pair of ears with a small pose variation. The probe ear is shown as the left image in (b), (c) and (d).

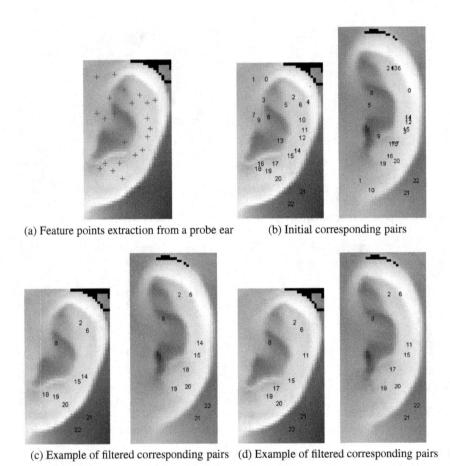

(a) Feature points extraction from a probe ear   (b) Initial corresponding pairs

(c) Example of filtered corresponding pairs   (d) Example of filtered corresponding pairs

Fig. 5.13. Example of grouping corresponding LSPs for a pair of ears with a large pose variation. The probe ear is shown on the left image in (b), (c) and (d).

5.3.1 Identification Performance

Every probe is matched to every 3D ear in the gallery set and the RMS registration error is calculated using the procedure described in Section 4.2. The matching error matrix $\{ME(i,j), i = 1, 2, \ldots, N_t, j = 1, 2, \ldots, N_m\}$ on the UCR dataset ES_1 using the LSP representation, where N_t and N_m are the number of probe ears and gallery ears, respectively, is displayed as an intensity image shown in Figure 5.14. The average time to match a pair of ears, which includes the coarse and fine alignment, is about 3.7 seconds with C++ implementation on a Linux machine with an *AMD Opteron* 1.8GHz CPU.

The identification performance is evaluated by the cumulative match characteristics (CMC). Table 5.3 shows the rank-r recognition rates using the LSP representation for the UCR dataset and the UND dataset Collection F. In Table 5.3, the numbers of images in the gallery and the probe sets are listed in the parenthesis following the name of the dataset. We achieve 94.84% rank-1 recognition rate (150 out of 155) on the UCR dataset ES_1 and 96.36% rank-1 recognition rate (291 out of 302) on the UND dataset Collection F. As expected, the system performs better on ES_1 with the same pose and the performance degrades slightly on ES_2 with pose variations.

We show four special cases of correctly recognizing gallery-probe ear pairs using the LSP representation in Figures 5.15. In this figure, each probe ear is rendered as a textured 3D surface and each gallery ear is displayed as a mesh. In order to examine the results visually, we display the pre-aligned gallery ear and the probe ear in the same image (Figures 5.15(b)) and also the post-aligned (transformed) gallery and the probe ear in the same image (Figures 5.15(c)). From Figure 5.15, we observe that the ear recognition system can handle partial occlusion. Twelve more examples of correctly recognized gallery-probe ear pairs are shown in Figure 5.16. From Figure 5.16, we observe that each gallery ear is well aligned with the corresponding probe ear.

One error case is illustrated in Figure 5.17. Figure 5.17 (a) and (b) show the color images of two visually similar probe and gallery ears that belong to different subjects; Figure 5.17(c) shows the corresponding gallery ear overlaid on the textured 3D probe ear after registration; Figure 5.17(d) shows the falsely recognized gallery ear overlaid on the textured 3D probe ear after alignment. In Figure 5.17(d), the root mean square error is 1.002mm, which is smaller than 1.079mm in

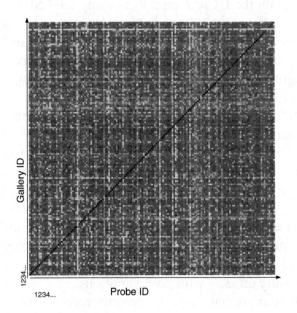

Fig. 5.14. Matching error matrix on the UCR dataset ES_1 using the LSP representation displayed as an intensity image (smaller values correspond to darker pixels). The gallery ID is labeled horizontally and the probe ID is labeled vertically.

Table 5.3. Cumulative matching performance on the UCR dataset and the UND dataset Collection F using the LSP representation.

Dataset	Rank-1	Rank-2	Rank-3	Rank-4	Rank-5
$UCR\ ES_1(155, 155)$	96.77%	96.77%	96.77%	96.77%	96.77%
$UCR\ ES_2(310, 592)$	94.43%	96.96%	97.30%	97.64%	97.80%
$UND(302, 302)$	96.36%	98.01%	98.34%	98.34%	98.34%

Figure 5.17(c). Since the ears of these two subjects are quite similar in 3D, the error occurs and it is an example of false recognition.

Figure 5.17 (a) and (b) show the color images of two visually similar probe and gallery ears that belong to different subjects; Figure 5.17(c) shows the true gallery ear overlaid on the textured 3D probe ear after registration; Figure 5.17(d) shows the falsely recognized gallery ear overlaid on the textured 3D probe ear after alignment. In Figure 5.17(d), the root mean square error for the falsely recognized ear is smaller than the error for the correct ear in Figure 5.17(c). Since we pick up the gallery ear with the minimum RMS error as the recognized ear, we made the errors. In this figure, we obtain good alignment between the gallery and model ears from different persons since these ears are quite similar in 3D.

5.3.2 Verification Performance

The verification performance of the proposed system is evaluated in terms of the two popular methods, the receiver operating characteristic (ROC) curve and the equal error rate (EER). Figure 5.18 shows the ROC curves on the UCR and the UND dataset Collection F using the LSP representation for surface matching. As expected, the system performs better on ES_1 than on ES_2 using the the LSP representations. We obtain the best performance with a 0.023 EER on the UND dataset using the LSP representation. It is clearly seen that without retuning the parameters of the proposed algorithms we achieved good verification performance on the UND dataset.

5.3.3 Evaluation of Verification Performance

We discuss and evaluate the accuracy of the ear verification system by applying the method in [38, 81, 82]. As described in Section 1.3, the UCR dataset has 155 subjects. There are 155 probes providing 155 user claims and 23,870 (155×154) imposter claims for the UCR dataset ES_1. For the UCR dataset ES_2 there are 592 probes providing 592 user claims and 91,168 (592×154) imposter claims. The UND dataset Collection F has 302 subjects. There are 302 pairs of images providing 302 user claims and 90,902 (302×301) imposter claims.

We calculate the number of user claims and imposter claims that gives statistically significant results. Let ζ_μ denote the $\mu-$percentile of

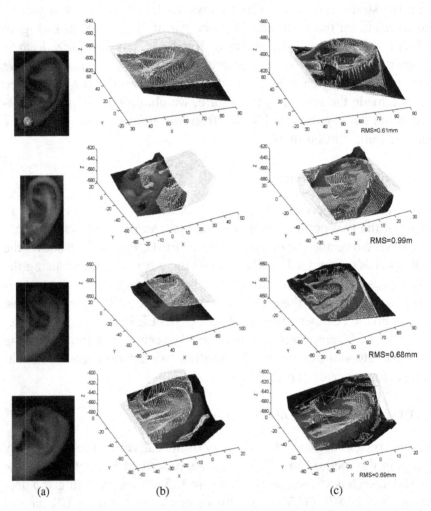

(a)   (b)   (c)

Fig. 5.15. UCR dataset: Four examples of the correctly recognized gallery-probe pairs using the LSP representation. Two ears have earrings and the other two ears are partially occluded by the hair. Images in column (a) show color images of ears. Images in column (b) and (c) show the probe ear with the corresponding gallery ear before the alignment and after the alignment, respectively. The gallery ears represented by the mesh are overlaid on the textured 3D probe ears. The units of x, y and z are in millimeters (mm).

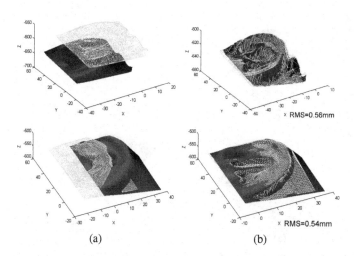

(a)   (b)

Fig. 5.16. UCR dataset: Twelve cases of the correctly recognized gallery-probe pairs using the LSP representation. (a) Examples of probe ears with the corresponding gallery ears before alignment. (b) Examples of probe ears with the correctly recognized gallery ears after alignment. The gallery ear represented by the mesh is overlaid on the textured 3D probe ear. The units of x, y and z are in millimeters (mm). Two example cases are shown on a page.

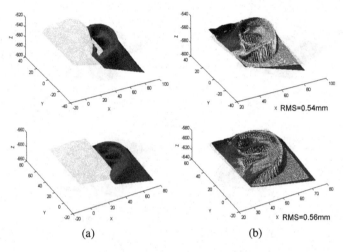

(a)   (b)

Fig. 5.16. Figure 5.16 Continued.

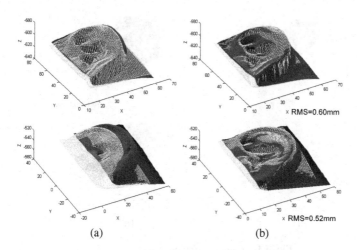

(a)   (b)

Fig. 5.16. Figure 5.16 Continued.

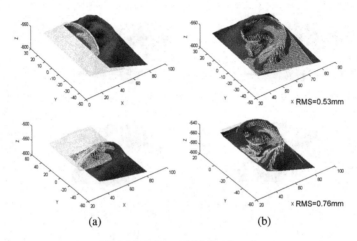

(a)   (b)

Fig. 5.16. Figure 5.16 Continued.

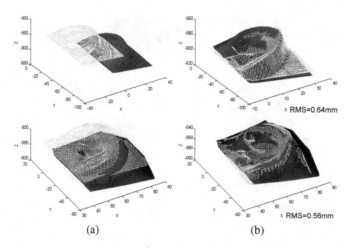

(a)   (b)

Fig. 5.16. Figure 5.16 Continued.

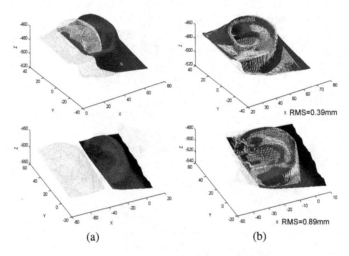

(a)   (b)

Fig. 5.16. Figure 5.16 Continued.

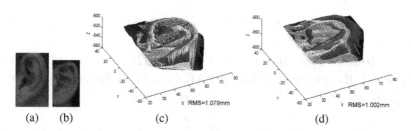

(a)   (b)   (c)   (d)

Fig. 5.17. UCR dataset: An incorrectly recognized model-test pair using the LSP representation. The model ear represented by the yellow mesh is overlaid on the textured 3D test ear. The units of x, y and z are in millimeters (mm). (a) Color image of the probe ear. (b) Color image of the falsely recognized gallery ear. (c) The gallery ear after alignment is overlaid on the texture 3D probe ear. (d) The falsely recognized gallery ear after alignment is overlaid on the textured 3D probe ear. Note that for the incorrect match the gallery ear in column (d) achieves a smaller value of RMS error than the gallery ear in column (c).

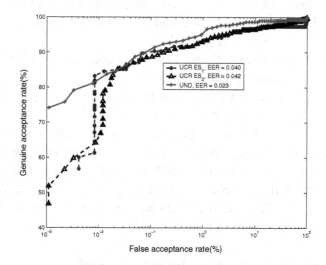

Fig. 5.18. UCR dataset and UND dataset Collection F: Verification performance as a ROC curve. ROC curves on the UCR dataset ES_1, ES_2 and the UND dataset using the LSP representation.

the standard Gaussian distribution with zero mean and unit variance. Since the verification tests can be thought of as Bernoulli trials, we can assert that with confidence $\delta = 1 - \mu$ that the minimum number of user claims which ensures that the expected value of FRR (p_{FR}) and the empirical value ($\widehat{p}_{FR}$) are related by $|p_{FR} - \widehat{p}_{FR}| \leq \xi$, is given by

$$v_C = \left(\frac{\zeta_{\mu/2}}{\xi}\right)^2 p_{FR}(1 - p_{FR}). \qquad (5.5)$$

The number v_I of the imposter claims [82] which is sufficient to ensure that the expected value of FAR (p_{FA}) and the empirical value ($\widehat{p}_{FA}$) are related by $|p_{FA} - \widehat{p}_{FA}| \leq \xi$ is given by

$$v_I = \left(\frac{\zeta_{\mu/2}}{\xi'}\right)^2 p_o(1 - p_o), \qquad \xi' = \frac{\xi}{k}, \qquad (1 - p_o)^k = 1 - p_{FA}$$
$$(5.6)$$

where p_o is the probability that one imposter is falsely accepted as an authorized user and k is the number of imposter claims ($k = 154$ for the UCR dataset and $k = 301$ for the UND dataset Collection F). By setting the desired EER, δ and ξ, we can compute v_C and v_I.

For the UCR dataset ES_1, we find $v_C = 149$ and $v_I = 24,759$ with $EER = 5\%$, $\delta = 95\%$ and $\xi = 3.5\%$.

For the UCR dataset ES_2, we find $v_C = 456$ and $v_I = 75,826$ with $EER = 5\%$, $\delta = 95\%$ and $\xi = 2\%$.

For the UND dataset Collection F, we find $v_C = 292$ and $v_I = 94,874$ with $EER = 5\%$, $\delta = 95\%$ and $\xi = 2.5\%$.

Note that the order of magnitude of these numbers are the same as those provided by the test scenarios. The values of ξ on the UCR dataset ES_2 ($\xi = 2\%$) and the UND dataset Collection F ($\xi = 2.5\%$) are smaller than the value on the UCR dataset ES_1 ($\xi = 3.5\%$) since the UCR dataset ES_2 and the UND dataset Collection F are larger in size than the size of the UCR dataset ES_1.

5.3.4 Comparison of LSP and Spin Image Representations

In order to compare the distinctive power of the LSP and the spin image representations, we follow the same procedures as described in this chapter to recognize ears using the spin image representation. In the experiments, the size of the spin image is 15×15. We perform experiments on the UCR dataset ES_1 (155 shots in the gallery and 155

shots in the probe) to compare the performance of these two representations in terms of the CMC and the ROC curves.

Table 5.4 shows CMC values using the LSP and the spin image
representations for ear recognition. Figure 5.19 shows the ROC curves
using the LSP and the spin image representations for matching ears.
From Table 5.4 and Figure 5.19, we observe that the LSP representation achieved a slightly better performance than the spin image representation.

5.3.5 Identification and Verification Performance with Occlusion

In order to show the recognition performance with occlusions, we sim-
ulate the occluded probe ear images by selecting a fraction of the extracted LSPs in the images. The area covered by the occluded LSPs is
removed. For a probe ear, we randomly remove 10%, 20%, 30%, 40%,
and 50% of the extracted LSPs and then match it against every ear
in the gallery. The identification performance is given in Table 5.5 and
the ROC curves for different occlusion ratios are shown in Figure 5.20.
We observe that the recognition performance degrades slowly with the
increased occlusion.

5.4 Comparison with Yan and Bowyer's Approach

The most important difference is that we propose the ear helix/anti-
helix and the local surface patch (LSP) representations to estimate the
initial rotation and translation between a gallery-probe pair while Yan
and Bowyer do not estimate the initial transformation. The initial transformation is critical for the success of ICP algorithm, which can be
seen from Table 5.6 that shows the rank-1 recognition rates. As described above, in the UND dataset Collection G, there are 24 subjects
whose images are taken at four different poses, straight-on, $15°$ off
center, $30°$ off center and $45°$ off center. For each angle of an ear image, we match it against all the images at different angles. This is the
same experiment performed in [34, Chap. 8.3]. We observe that the results obtained by the helix/anti-helix representation are better than Yan
and Bowyer's results [34, Chap. 8.3] for all the cases except the case
($45°$ probe against $30°$ gallery). The results obtained by the LSP representation outperform the results obtained in [34, Chap. 8.3] for the

Table 5.4. Cumulative matching performance on the UCR dataset ES_1 using the LSP and the spin image representations.

Representation	Rank-1	Rank-2	Rank-3	Rank-4	Rank-5
LSP	94.84%	96.77%	96.77%	96.77%	96.77%
Spin Image	92.90%	95.48%	95.48%	95.48%	95.48%

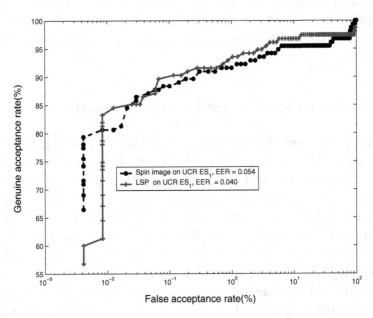

Fig. 5.19. Verification performance as ROC curves using the LSP and the spin image representations on the UCR dataset ES_1.

Table 5.5. Cumulative matching performance on the UCR dataset ES_1 with different occlusion ratios using the LSP representation.

Occlusion ratio	Rank-1	Rank-2	Rank-3	Rank-4	Rank-5
0	94.84%	96.77%	96.77%	96.77%	96.77%
0.1	94.19%	96.13%	96.13%	96.13%	96.13%
0.2	92.26%	94.84%	94.84%	95.48%	95.48%
0.3	90.97%	92.90%	92.90%	94.19%	95.48%
0.4	87.74%	92.90%	92.90%	92.90%	93.55%
0.5	84.52%	88.39%	88.39%	88.39%	88.39%

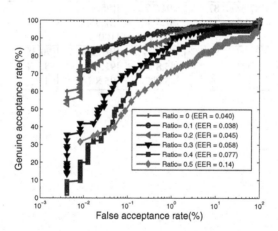

Fig. 5.20. Verification performance as ROC curves with different occlusion ratios on the UCR dataset ES_1 using the LSP representation.

Table 5.6. Comparison between Chen and Bhanu's approach [1] and Yan and Bowyer's approach [2] on a subset of Collection G. Our rank-1 identification results are put inside the brackets. The first number is obtained using the helix/anti-helix representation and the second one is obtained using the LSP representation. The number outside the bracket is obtained from [34, Chap. 8.3].

Probe\Gallery	Straight-on	15° off	30° off	45° off	Average
Straight-on		[100%, 100%], 100%	[91.7%, 87.5%], 87.5%	[87.5%, 83.3%], 70.8%	[93.1%, 90.3%], 86.1%
15° off	[100%, 100%], 100%		[100%, 100%], 100%	[87.5%, 91.7%], 87.5%	[95.8%, 97.2%], 95.8%
30° off	[91.7%, 91.7%], 87.5%	[100%, 100%], 100%		[95.8%, 91.7%], 95.8%	[95.8%, 94.4%], 94.4%
45° off	[87.5%, 87.5%], 79.2%	[91.7%, 87.5%], 87.5%	[95.8%, 87.5%], 100%		[91.7%, 87.5%], 88.9%
Average	[93.1%, 93.1%], 88.9%	[95.8%, 95.8%], 95.8%	[97.2%, 91.7%], 95.8%	[90.3%, 88.9%], 84.7%	[94.1%, 92.4%], 91.3%

cases with large pose variations (45° and 30° probes against straight-on gallery, straight-on and 15° probes against 45° gallery). From Table 5.6, we see that our representations can reasonably handle the pose variation up to 45°.

5.5 Conclusions

In this chapter, we proposed a new local surface patch (LSP) representation for 3D matching. This representation is invariant to rotation and translation. We used this representation for finding initial correspondences between a gallery-probe pair. Then a modified iterative closest point (ICP) algorithm iteratively refined the transformation which brings the hypothesized gallery and a probe image into the best alignment. The root mean square (RMS) registration error is used as the matching error criterion. The experimental results on two real ear range and color image datasets demonstrated the potential of the proposed algorithms for robust ear recognition in 3D. Extensive experiments are performed on the UCR dataset (155 subjects with 902 images under pose variations), the UND dataset Collection F (302 subjects with 302 time-lapse gallery-probe pairs) and a subset of the UND dataset G for evaluating the performance with respect to pose variations without retuning the parameters of the proposed algorithms. These results showed that the proposed ear recognition system is capable of recognizing ears under pose variations, partial occlusions and time lapse effects. The proposed representation is less sensitive to pose variations.

We also provided a comparison of the LSP representation with the spin image representation for identification and verification. This comparison showed that the LSP representation achieved a slightly better performance than the spin image representation.

6

Rapid 3D Ear Indexing and Recognition

In this chapter, we proposes a novel method that combines the feature embedding for the fast retrieval of surface descriptors, novel similarity measures for correspondences, and a support vector machine (SVM)-based learning technique for ranking the hypotheses. The local surface patch (LSP) representation is used to find the correspondence between a model-test pair. Due to its high dimensionality, an embedding algorithm is used that maps the feature vectors to a low-dimensional space where distance relationships are preserved. By searching the nearest neighbors in low dimensions, the similarity between a model-test pair is computed using the novel features. The similarities for all model-test pairs are ranked using the learning algorithm to generate a short list of candidate models for verification. The verification is performed by aligning a model with the test object.

6.1 Introduction

In this chapter, we discuss the problem of recognizing 3D objects from 3D range images. Various techniques have been proposed for 3D object recognition and indexing; for instance, geometric hashing and surface descriptor matching [51]. However, most of the research has focused on the recognition of 3D dissimilar objects using a small database. It is desired to design a scalable and efficient 3D object recognition system.

In this chapter, we present a new framework that handles the recognition of highly similar 3D objects with a good scalability performance on large databases. We improve the local surface patch (LSP) descriptor originally proposed by Bhanu and Chen [12] and it has been shown to be more effective and efficient than the popular spin image and spherical spin image representations [1, 3, 83]. We develop an efficient framework based on the improved LSP representation but any other surface representations such as the spin image can be used. The core component of a LSP descriptor is a 2D histogram, whose dimensionality is large (in hundreds). Search of the closest LSPs in a high-dimensional space is time consuming. Further, most of the current 3D object recognition systems identify objects by matching a test object to every model object. This is definitely not efficient and geometric hashing kinds of techniques have been popular in computer vision. In our proposed approach, we combine the feature embedding for the fast retrieval of surface descriptors and the SVM technique for ranking the hypotheses to generate a short list for the verification.

Campbell and Flynn [51] provided a comprehensive survey on 3D free-form object recognition. In this chapter the review is focused on the 3D object recognition using indexing techniques. Geometric hashing has been a popular technique used for generating the hypotheses [52, 53, 58]. However the experiments on a small dataset ($\sim$20 objects) of dissimilar objects are performed and the time and space complexity of hashing is polynomial in the number of feature points. The related work is summarized in Table 6.1.

The main contributions of this chapter are: (1) A novel computational framework is presented that integrates feature embedding and rank learning for efficient recognition of 3D highly similar objects.Such an integration has not been done before. (2) The performance of the proposed algorithm is scalable with the database size without sacrificing much accuracy. (3) No assumptions about the distributions of features is made as has been done in [84]. (4) Extensive experiments on two real large datasets are presented and compared with the geometric hashing to show the effectiveness of the approach.

6.2 Indexing Approach

The system diagram is illustrated in Figure 6.1. Given a model object, we extract the feature points that are defined as either the local minimum or the local maximum of shape index values. Then we calculate local surface patch (LSP) descriptors for the feature points and their neighbors. A "local surface patch" is defined as the region consisting

Table 6.1. 3D object recognition from range images using indexing techniques.

Authors	Technique	Database
Yi and Chelberg [59]	Bayesian framework to achieve efficient indexing.	20 objects
Johnson and Hebert [3]	Used the principal component analysis (PCA) to compress the surface descriptors, the spin images.	20 objects
Matei et al. [84]	Combined the locality sensitive hashing [85] for approximate nearest neighbor search and the joint 3D-signature estimation for generation and evaluation of alignment hypotheses.	Two non-publicly available vehicle databases (89 and 366 objects)
Mokhtarian et al. [58]	Used geometric hashing for the generation of hypotheses.	20 objects
Stein and Medioni [52]	Used geometric hashing for the generation of hypotheses.	9 objects
Chen and Bhanu [57]	Used geometric hashing for the generation of hypotheses.	9 objects
Muller et al. [86]	Incorporated spatio-temporal invariance into the geometric features and proposed efficient indexing methods.	Synthetic motion capture data (Not the 3D range data)
This chapter	A novel method that combines the feature embedding, local structural similarity measures and rank learning techniques.	Two public databases of highly similar objects (155 and 302 objects)

of a feature point and its neighbors. The LSP representation includes a feature point, its surface type (convex/concave/saddle), the centroid of the patch and a 2D histogram of shape index values vs. dot product of the surface normal at the feature point and its neighbors [1]. Based on the surface type of a LSP, a LSP is classified into three types (convex/concave/saddle). For each type of LSP, we apply a feature embedding algorithm to embed the original feature vector (the 2D histogram of a LSP is concatenated into a feature vector) into a low-dimensional space such that the distance relationships are preserved. The K-d tree structure is used to perform the search in the low-dimensional space. Given a test image, we repeat the same procedures to map LSPs into the corresponding low-dimensional embedded space based on its surface type. By searching the nearest neighbors of the embedded feature vectors, we find the potential corresponding local surface patches between a model-test pair. The initial correspondences are filtered and grouped to remove false correspondences using geometric constraints.

Based on the set of correspondences, a set of features is computed to measure the similarity between the model-test pair. Then the hypotheses are ranked using the rank learning algorithm to generate a short list of candidate models for verification. The parameters of the SVM classifier are learned on a subset of the database. For verification, we perform surface matching by applying the iterative closest point (ICP) algorithm in which the initial transformation is obtained from the corresponding LSPs.

6.3 Local Surface Patch Representation

We choose local surface patch (LSP) representation as the surface descriptor. The LSP descriptor has been shown to be effective and distinctive for recognizing 3D similar objects [1, 83]. A local surface patch is described by a 2D histogram, surface type and the centroid. The 2D histogram and surface type are used for comparison of LSPs and the centroid is used for computing the rigid transformation. The patch encodes the geometric information of a local surface.

Since the LSP representation is described by a histogram, the χ^2-divergence and earth movers distance (EMD) [87] are two proper distances. However the χ^2-divergence is non-metric and EMD is computationally expensive, we choose Euclidean distance to measure the distance between two descriptors.

6.3.1 Feature Embedding

Given a query feature vector in a high-dimensional space, searching its closest matches in a large database is time consuming. Various methods have been proposed to speed up the nearest-neighbor retrieval, including hashing and tree structures. However, the complexity of these methods grows exponentially with the increase in dimensionality. In recent years, a number of approaches, which *embed* feature vectors in a high-dimensional space into a low-dimensional space, have been proposed [88–94]. Multidimensional scaling (MDS) [89], LLE [88] and ISOMAP [90] cannot handle online query efficiently. Lipschitz embedding [91], FastMap [92], MetricMap [93] and BoostMap [94] can efficiently handle online query.

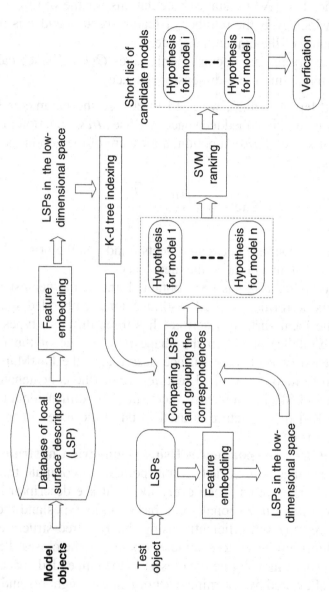

Fig. 6.1. System diagram for rapid 3D ear recognition.

As compared to the above algorithms which can handle online query, *FastMap* has the following attractive advantages:

- It only needs $O(Nk)$ distance calculations for the offline embedding in which N is the number of feature vectors and k is the dimensionality of the embedded space.
- Given a query feature vector, it only takes $O(k)$ distance calculations to map it into the k-dimensional space.

For the fastMap algorithm, we need to choose the parameter k, the dimensionality of the embedded space. We use *Stress* function to guide the choice of k. The *Stress* function, a measure of the goodness-of-fit, is defined as

$$\text{Stress} = \sqrt{\frac{(d'_{ij} - d_{ij})^2}{\sum_{ij} d_{ij}^2}} \qquad (6.1)$$

where d_{ij} is the distance between objects i and j in the original space and d'_{ij} is the distance in the embedded space.

Once the embedding has been obtained, the actual nearest neighbor search is performed in the low-dimensional embedded space. In our case, the local surface descriptor has three different types (convex/concave/saddle) based on the shape index value of the feature point. For each type of local surface descriptors, the FastMap algorithm is run to map the original feature vector (the concatenated 2D histogram of a LSP) into a feature vector in a low-dimensional feature space. The K-d tree structure is used to build the index in the low-dimensional space.

1) **Forming Correspondences Using Geometric Constraints**

Given a test image, we extract feature points and compute the local surface patch descriptors. Then every local surface descriptor is embedded into a low-dimensional space based on its types and the similar LSPs are retrieved efficiently using the K-d tree structure. The FastMap algorithm introduces some errors in that the closest LSPs in the original space may not be the closest in the embedded space. This problem is alleviated by returning a set of nearest neighbors and using the geometric constraints to group the correspondences.

The potential corresponding LSP pairs are filtered and grouped based on the geometric constraints which are illustrated in Figure 6.2.

$$d_{C_1,C_2} = |d_{L_t^i,L_t^j} - d_{L_m^i,L_m^j}| < \epsilon_2$$
$$\max(d_{L_t^i,L_t^j}, d_{L_m^i,L_m^j}) > \epsilon_3$$
$$(|\alpha - \alpha'|, |\beta - \beta'|, |\gamma - \gamma'|) < \epsilon_4 \qquad (6.2)$$

where $d_{L_t^i,L_t^j}$ and $d_{L_m^i,L_m^j}$ are the Euclidean distances between the centroids of the two surface patches. In equation (6.2), α is the angle between the surface normals at the feature points of the two surface patches (L_t^i, L_t^j); β is the angle between the surface normal of the patch L_t^i and the line connected by the centroids of the two patches (L_t^i, L_t^j); γ is the angle between the surface normal of the patch L_t^j and the line connected by the centroids of the two patches (L_t^i, L_t^j). α', β' and γ' are defined in the same way.

The first distance constraint and the following three orientation constraints guarantee that the two corresponding pairs (L_t^i, L_t^j) and (L_m^i, L_m^j) are consistent; the second constraint removes the correspondences which are too close. We use these geometric constraints to partition the potential corresponding pairs into different groups. The larger the group is, the more likely it contains the true corresponding pairs. Given a list of corresponding pairs, the grouping procedure for every pair in the list is as follows.

- Initialize each pair of a group.
- For every group, add other pairs to it if they satisfy (6.2).
- Repeat the same procedure for every group.
- Sort the groups in the ascending order based on the size of groups.
- Select the groups on the top of the list.

2) Computing Similarities
Once we find the n corresponding pairs $\{L_m^i, L_t^i\}, i = 1, 2, \cdots, n$ where L_t^i is the ith local surface descriptor and L_m^i is its correspondence in the model m, we compute seven features to measure the similarity between them. The seven features are computed based on the following equations.

$$\text{ratio} = \frac{n}{N_t}$$

$$e_1 = \sqrt{\frac{1}{n}\sum_{i=1}^{n}(f_c(L_t^i) - T(f_c(L_m^i)))^2}$$

$$e_2 = \rho\sum_{i=1}^{n}\sum_{j=1,j\neq i}^{n}(d(f_c(L_t^i), f_c(L_t^j))$$

$$- d(f_c(L_m^i), f_c(L_m^j)))^2$$

$$e_3 = \frac{1}{n}\sum_{i=1}^{n}(f_n(L_t^i) \bullet T(f_n(L_m^i)))$$

$$e_4 = \rho\sum_{i=1}^{n}\sum_{j=1,j\neq i}^{n}(|\alpha_{ij} - \alpha'_{ij}|)$$

$$e_5 = \rho\sum_{i=1}^{n}\sum_{j=1,j\neq i}^{n}(|\beta_{ij} - \beta'_{ij}|)$$

$$e_6 = \rho\sum_{i=1}^{n}\sum_{j=1,j\neq i}^{n}(|\gamma_{ij} - \gamma'_{ij}|) \qquad (6.3)$$

In equation (6.3), the notations are explained below.

- N_t is the number of local surface descriptors in the scene;
- T is the rigid transformation obtained from the n correspondences which aligns the model and test and $\bullet$ denotes the dot product;
- $\rho = \frac{2}{n(n-1)}$; $d(\cdot)$ is the Euclidean distance between two 3D coordinates;
- $f_c(L_i)$ gets the 3D coordinates of the LSP L_i;
- f_n gets the surface normal vector of the LSP L_i.
- The *ratio* counts the fraction of local surface descriptors in the scene which find the correspondences;
- e_1 is the registration error;
- e_2 is the average pairwise distance between the corresponding LSPs;
- e_3 measures the average distance between the surface normal vectors of a corresponding LSP pair;
- e_4, e_5 and e_6 are the pairwise angle difference between the corresponding LSPs.

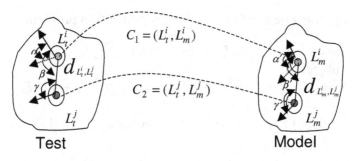

Fig. 6.2. Geometric constraints for grouping LSPs.

6.3.2 Ranking the Hypotheses Using SVM

In [84] a *posterior* probability of a model, given the scene surface descriptors, model surface descriptors and the alignment parameter, is computed to rank the candidate models. In order to compute the *posterior* probability, several assumptions are made, for instance, the uniform distribution of a model, the independence of the scene surface descriptors and the Gaussian distribution of the residuals. These assumptions may not hold in the real data.

In our case, given a test, we compute a set of features as a measure of the similarity for every model in the database. We would like to rank the candidate models in the descending order based on these features without making any assumptions. We use a support vector machine (SVM) approach to learn the ranking function, which makes use of the two advantages of SVM, "large-margin" and "kernel trick" for supporting the nonlinear ranking [95].

The problem of ranking is formalized as follows. For a query q and a collection of documents $D = \{d_1, d_2, \cdots, d_m\}$, we say $d_i <_r d_j$ or $(d_i, d_j) \in r$ if d_i is ranked higher than d_j for an ordering r. Using the techniques of SVM, the ranking function f can be learned from the training data. Assume the ranking function is linear such that: $(d_i, d_j) \in f_{\mathbf{w}(q)} \iff \mathbf{w}^T \phi(q, d_i) > \mathbf{w}^T \phi(q, d_j)$ in which $\mathbf{w}$ is a weight vector adjusted by learning and $\phi(q, d)$ is a mapping onto features that describe the match between query q and document d.

In our case, $\phi(q, d)$ is the feature vector consisting of the seven feature computed as a measure of the similarity between q and d. The task of the learner is to minimize the number of discordant ranking pairs. Though this problem is known to be NP-hard, the solution is approximated by introducing non-negative slack variables $\xi_{i,j,k}$. Therefore, the problem is converted to the following optimization problem.

$$\text{minimize:} \quad V(\mathbf{w}, \xi) = \tfrac{1}{2}\mathbf{w}^T \cdot \mathbf{w} + C\sum \xi_{i,j,k}$$

subject to:

$$\forall(d_i, d_j) \in r_1^* : \mathbf{w}^T\phi(q_1, d_i) \geq \mathbf{w}^T\phi(q_1, d_j) + 1 - \xi_{i,j,1}$$

$$\cdots \qquad\qquad\qquad\qquad\qquad\qquad\qquad\qquad (6.4)$$

$$\forall(d_i, d_j) \in r_n^* : \mathbf{w}^T\phi(q_n, d_i) \geq \mathbf{w}^T\phi(q_n, d_j) + 1 - \xi_{i,j,n}$$

$$\forall_i\forall_j\forall_k : \xi_{i,j,k} \geq 0$$

C is a parameter that controls the trade off between the margin size and training error. By rearranging the constraints in (6.4) as $\mathbf{w}^T(\phi(q_k, d_i) - \phi(q_k, d_i)) \geq 1 - \xi_{i,j,k}$, it becomes equivalent to that of SVM classification on pairwise difference vectors $(\phi(q_k, d_i) - \phi(q_k, d_i))$.

In the training stage, given a test object, its corresponding model should be ranked in the top. We do not care the relative rankings of other model objects. For each test-model pair, we compute the seven features as a measure of the similarity between them (described in Section 6.3.1). We also know the ranking order of the model objects. Therefore, this training data is input to the SVM learning algorithm to learn the optimal ranking function. Given a test q, the model objects can be sorted in the descending order based on the value of $rsv(q, d_i) = \mathbf{w}^{*T}\phi(q, d_i) = \sum \alpha_{k,l}^*\phi(q_k, d_l)^T\phi(q, d_i)$, where $\alpha_{k,l}^*$ is derived from the values of the dual variables at the solution. As a result, the $\varsigma\%$ of the models on the top of sorted list are selected for the verification.

6.4 Verification

After the initial rigid transformation is estimated from the corresponding pairs between a model-test pair, the Iterative Closest Point (ICP) algorithm [63] is run to refine the transformation which brings the model and test into the best alignment. The basic steps of the modified ICP algorithm are the same as described in Section 4.2.2.

Starting with the initial transformation, the modified ICP algorithm is run to refine the transformation by minimizing the distance between the control points of the model and their closest points of the test object. For every model in the short list picked up by the SVM rank learning algorithm, the control points are randomly selected and the modified ICP is applied to those points. For a selected model object, we repeat the same procedure N_r times and choose the rigid transformation with the minimum root mean square (RMS) error. The model in the database with the minimum RMS error is declared as the recognized object. In the modified ICP algorithm, the speed bottleneck is the nearest neighbor search. Therefore, the K-d tree structure is used in the implementation.

6.5 Experimental Results

We apply the proposed framework, which combines the feature embedding and rank learning, to recognize highly similar 3D objects. We perform extensive experiments on two publicly available large 3D ear databases, UND dataset Collection F (302 subjects with 604 shots) and UCR dataset (155 subjects with 902 shots), to demonstrate the effectiveness of the approach. All the times reported in the following are measured *in seconds* on a Linux machine with an *AMD Opteron* 1.8 GHz processor.

6.5.1 Dimensionality of the Embedding

As described in Section 6.3.1, the *Stress* is used to determine the dimensionality k of the embedded space. We perform experiments on a subset of the UCR dataset and compute the *Stress* with respect to different k. The results are shown in Table 6.2. The similar results are obtained on the UND dataset. We observe that the *Stress* decreases as k increases. However, the "curse of dimensionality" is a problem for the K-d tree; we choose $k = 24$ for the two datasets.

For different k, we show the times for searching the nearest neighbors with and without feature embedding on the UND dataset and the UCR dataset in Table 6.3. We see that the speed of searching the nearest neighbors in the embedded space is directly proportional to the dimensionality k. Since we select $k = 24$, it results in a speed up of approximately 90 times compared with using the sequential search in the original feature space.

6.5.2 Correspondence Using the Geometric Constraints

Once the LSPs are embedded in the low-dimensional space, the correspondences are obtained by searching the nearest neighbors which

Table 6.2. The relation between *Stress* and k.

k	12	16	20	24
Stress	0.351	0.312	0.277	0.246

Table 6.3. The time in seconds for searching the nearest neighbors with and without feature embedding on the UND and UCR datasets. The first number is on the UND dataset (480,000 LSPs) and the second one is on the UCR dataset (300,000 LSPs)

No embedding		(985.4, 93.5)			
With embedding	k	12	16	20	24
	Time	4.69, 0.47	7.1, 0.71	9.27, 0.82	11.1, 1.06
	Speed up	210, 199	139, 122	106, 114	89, 88

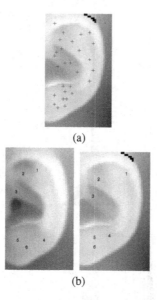

(a)

(b)

Fig. 6.3. Example of grouping for corresponding LSPs for a pair of ears. (a) Feature points marked by plus signs extracted from a test ear. (b) Corresponding pairs between the test-model pair obtained by applying the geometric constraints (6.2). In (b), the model ear is shown on the left side.

are filtered by the geometric constraints. Figure 6.3 shows one example of recovered correspondences. Figure 6.3(a) shows the feature point extraction results marked by the red pluses for a test ear; Figure 6.3(b) shows the recovered correspondences, in which every pair is represented by the same number superimposed on the test and model images. We can see that the true corresponding pairs are obtained by searching the nearest neighbors and using the geometric constraints. Each group of the correspondences belongs to either the matched pairs or the non-matched pairs. For each of them, we compute seven features as a measure of the similarity between a pair. The distributions of features are shown in Figures 6.4 and 6.5. If a Bayesian classifier is used to classify a group either from matched pair or non-matched pair, it may not work well since the feature distributions for matched and non-matched pairs have a large overlap, which can be clearly observed in Figures 6.4 and 6.5. Instead, the SVM rank learning algorithm is used to rank the candidate models based on the seven features without making any assumption about the feature distributions.

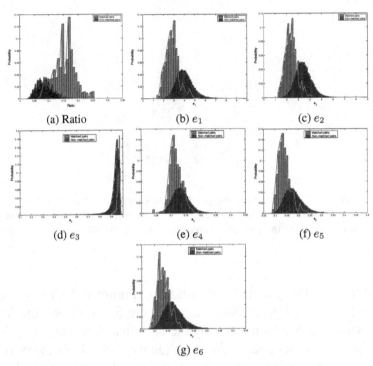

(a) Ratio   (b) e_1 (c) e_2

(d) e_3 (e) e_4 (f) e_5

(g) e_6

Fig. 6.4. UND dataset: Distributions of the seven features for the matched and non-matched pairs. This figure is best viewed in color.

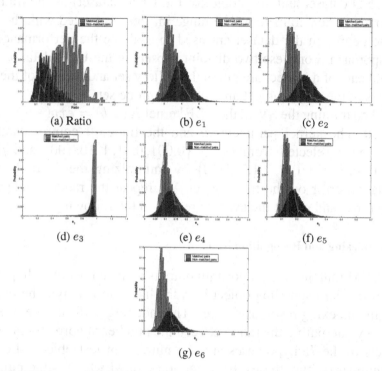

(a) Ratio   (b) e_1 (c) e_2

(d) e_3 (e) e_4 (f) e_5

(g) e_6

Fig. 6.5. UCR dataset: Distributions of the seven features for the matched and non-matched pairs. This figure is best viewed in color.

6.5.3 SVM Rank Learning Algorithm

To evaluate the performance of the approach, each of the two dataset is divided into disjoint subsets for training and testing. For the SVM rank learning, we randomly select 30% of the subjects (90 people for the UND dataset and 46 people for the UCR dataset) as the training set to learn the parameters. The range images associated with the rest of the people in the dataset are used to evaluate the performance of the approach. For these two disjoint subsets in the UCR dataset, two frontal ears of a subject are put in the gallery set and the rest of the ear images of the same subject are put in the probe set.

When training the SVM, the RBF kernel $K(a, b) = exp(-\mu |a-b|^2)$ is used. The kernel parameter μ and the trade-off control parameter C were selected from $C \in \{0.001, 0.01, 1, 10, 100\}$ and $\mu \in \{0.001, 0.01, 0.1, 0.5, 1, 1.5, 4, 16\}$ by minimizing the 10-fold cross validation error on the training set. We repeat the random selection three times and report the average results in the following.

6.5.4 Indexing and Recognition Results

The SVM rank learning algorithm outputs a ranked list of H hypotheses. If the corresponding object is in the list of top H hypotheses, we take the indexing result as correct. The indexing performance is evaluated by computing the ratio between the number of correctly indexed objects in the H hypotheses and the number of test objects. Let H, the number of hypotheses, be a fraction ς of M which is the number of models in the database, we calculate the indexing performance and perform the verification for the picked ς candidate models. The indexing and recognition results are listed in Table 6.4. We observe that 94% of the objects are correctly indexed with a list of 30% of model objects in the database as hypotheses on the two datasets. The relative large number of models retrieved is due to the high degree of similarity between model objects.

The average recognition time for a test and the recognition performance are tabulated in Table 6.5 under three cases:

- Case (1): matching a test with every model object in the database without the feature embedding;
- Case (2): matching a test with every model object in the database with the feature embedding;

- Case (3): matching a test only with the 30% candidate models picked from the ranked list with the feature embedding and SVM rank learning.

We see that the recognition time per test with the feature embedding and rank learning is reduced by a factor of 6.6 with the 2.4% recognition performance on the UND dataset; and on the UCR dataset the time is reduced by a factor of 6 with the degradation of 5.8% in recognition performance. This could be reduced if we embed the LSPs into a higher-dimensional space. We notice that the average recognition time per test is longer on the UND dataset than that on the UCR dataset since the UND dataset has a higher resolution and it has a larger number of LSPs. From Table 6.4 and Table 6.5, we also observe that the indexing and recognition performances on the UND dataset is better since the UCR dataset has more pose variations.

Figure 6.6 shows three examples of the correctly recognized model-test ear pairs. Figure 6.6(a) shows the model ear and the test ear before alignment; Figure 6.6(b) shows the model ear and the test ear after alignment. We observe that the model ear is aligned well with the test.

During the recognition, some errors are made and the two error cases are illustrated in Figure 6.7. Figure 6.7(a) and (b) show the range images of two visually similar test and model ears that belong to different subjects; Figure 6.7(c) shows the true model ear overlaid on the 3D test ear after registration; Figure 6.7(d) shows the falsely recognized model ear overlaid on the 3D test ear after alignment. In Figure 6.7(d), the root mean square error for the falsely recognized ear is smaller than the error for the correct ear in Figure 6.7(c). In this figure, we obtain good alignment between the model and test ears from different persons since these ears are quite similar in 3D.

6.5.5 Effect of Feature Embedding

We would like to evaluate the effect of the feature embedding on the verification performance for the above first two cases (see Table 6.5) with sequential matching. Therefore, we perform experiments on the first two cases and demonstrate the verification performance using the receiver operating characteristic (ROC) curve and the equal error rate (EER). The ROC curve is the plot of genuine acceptance rate (GAR) versus the corresponding false acceptance rate (FAR). GAR is defined

Table 6.4. The indexing and recognition performance on the UND and UCR datasets. The first bracket is on the UND dataset and the second one is on the UCR dataset. The first number in the bracket is the indexing performance and the second one is the recognition performance.

ς(Fraction of dataset)	Performance
0.5%	[53.3%, 53.3%], [61.7%, 61.7%]
5%	[82.54%, 81.6%], [81.72%, 81.55%]
10%	[87.74%, 87.74%], [87.41%, 85.19%]
15%	[91.51%, 90.09%], [90.69%, 87.38%]
20%	[92.92%, 92.92%], [91.89%, 88.83%]
25%	[94.39%, 93.87%], [93.34%, 90.53%]
30%	[94.81%, 94.34%], [94.38%, 90.78%]
35%	[95.75%, 94.81%], [95.35%, 91.26%]

Table 6.5. The recognition time and performance on three cases for the UND and UCR datasets. The first number in the parenthesis is on the UND dataset and the second one is on the UCR dataset. Please see the text for the description of the three cases.

	Case 1	Case 2	Case 3
Time per test	(1270, 436)	(400, 215)	(192, 72)
Recognition rate	(96.7, 96.4)	(96.7, 94.9)	(94.3, 90.8)

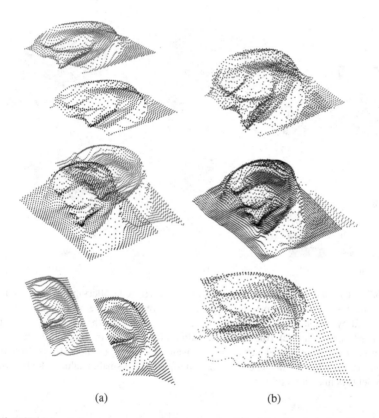

(a)   (b)

Fig. 6.6. UCR dataset: three cases of correctly recognized model-test pairs using the proposed algorithm. Each row shows one case. The model ears represented by the red pluses are overlaid on the test ears represented by the black dots. (a) Model (plus signs) and test (dots) ears before alignment. (b) Model and test ears after alignment. In case 1, the rotation angle is $12.7°$ and the axis is $[0.4566, \ -0.8561, \ 0.2423]^T$. In case 2, the rotation angle is $20.3°$ and the axis is $[-0.0204, \ -0.9972, \ 0.0713]^T$. In case 3, the rotation angle is $25.4°$ and the axis is $[-0.0496, 0.9970, \ -0.0598]^T$.

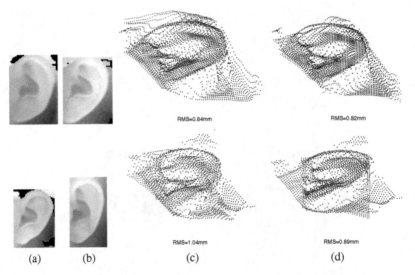

RMS=0.84mm   RMS=0.82mm

RMS=1.04mm   RMS=0.89mm

(a)   (b)   (c)   (d)

Fig. 6.7. UCR dataset: two cases of incorrectly recognized gallery-probe pairs. Each row shows one case. The model ears represented by the red pluses are overlaid on the test ears represented by the black dots. (a) Range images of the test ears. (b) Range images of falsely recognized model ears. (c) True model ears after alignment are overlaid on the test ears. (d) The falsely recognized model ears after alignment are overlaid on the test ears. Note that for the incorrect matches the model ears in column (d) achieve a smaller value of RMS error than the model ears in column (c).

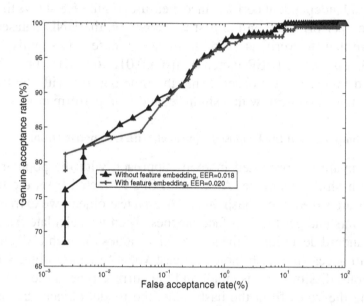

Fig. 6.8. UND dataset: verification performance for the first two cases in Table 6.5.

Table 6.6. Comparison of the proposed approach with geometric hashing (GH) in terms of the indexing performance and the search time (in seconds) for the nearest neighbors. The first number in the parenthesis is on the UND dataset and the second one is on the UCR dataset.

	Indexing Performance		Time	
ς	This Chapter	GH	This Chapter	GH
0.5%	(53.3%, 61.7%)	(1.65%, 32.7%)		
5%	(82.54%, 81.72%)	(23.59%, 57.68%)		
10%	(87.74%, 87.41%)	(35.61%, 69.93%)		
15%	(91.51%, 90.69%)	(45.99%, 76.49%)	(11.1,	(9.6,
20%	(92.92%, 91.89%)	(53.77%, 81.55%)	1.06)	0.54)
25%	(94.39%, 93.34%)	(59.67%, 85.88%)		
30%	(94.81%, 94.38%)	(64.39%, 89.57%)		
35%	(95.75%, 95.35%)	(69.33%, 91.42%)		

as the percentage of the occurrences that an authorized user is correctly accepted by the system, while FAR is defined as the percentage of the occurrences that a non-authorized user is falsely accepted by the system. The EER, which indicates the rate at which false rejection rate ($FRR = 1 - GAR$) and the false acceptance rate are equal, is a threshold independent performance measure. Figure 6.8 shows the verification performance on the first two cases on the UND dataset. We observe that the verification performance in case 2 is slightly worse than that in case 1 (EER increases from 0.018 to 0.020). From Table 6.5 and Figure 6.8 we observe that the time per test with the feature embedding is reduced with a slight reduction in performance.

6.5.6 Comparison of the Proposed Appraoch with Geometric Hashing

We compare the proposed indexing approach with the popular geometric hashing technique. All of the LSPs extracted from the model objects are saved into a hash table. Given a test object, we extract feature points and get local surface patches. Then we calculate the mean and standard deviation of the shape index values for each LSP and use them to access the hash table and cast votes to model objects if the histogram dissimilarity is small and the surface type is the same. By tallying the votes from the hash table, the model objects are ranked in the descending order based on the votes they received. We perform the experiments described in Section 6.5.4 on the same datasets. The comparison results with geometric hashing are listed in Table 6.6. We observe that the indexing performance of the proposed approach outperforms the geometric hashing on the two datasets. Although the search time for the nearest neighbors using geometric hashing on the UCR dataset is about half of the time using the proposed approach, there is not much difference (9.6 vs. 11.1) in time on the UND dataset since the UND dataset contains a larger number of LSPs. We also notice that the geometric hashing performs poorly on the UND dataset since a larger number of LSPs in this dataset increase the chances of collisions caused by the keys hashing to the same index.

6.6 Conclusions

In this chapter, we have presented a general framework for efficient recognition of highly similar 3D object that combines the feature embedding and SVM rank learning techniques. Unlike the previous work for fast object recognition in 3D range images, we achieved a sublinear time complexity on the number of models without making any assumptions about the feature distributions. Experimental results on two large real datasets containing highly similar objects in shape confirmed the effectiveness and efficiency of the proposed framework. Furthermore, a comparison with the geometric hashing shows that the proposed approach performs much better. Considering the fact that the two datasets used here contain a large number of very similar 3D objects, the proposed approach is promising, in general, for 3D object recognition.

7

Performance Prediction of a 3D Ear Recognition System

Existing ear recognition approaches do not provide any theoretical or experimental performance prediction. Therefore, the discriminating power of ear biometrics for human identification cannot be evaluated. In this chapter, a binomial model is presented to predict the ear recognition performance. Match and non-match distances obtained from matching 3D ears are used to estimate their distributions. By modeling cumulative match characteristic (CMC) curve as a binomial distribution, the ear recognition performance can be predicted on a larger gallery.

7.1 Introduction

As we have seen in Chapter 2 in recent years, many approaches have been developed for ear recognition from 2D or 3D images [1, 2, 9–19, 34]. However, these ear recognition approaches do not provide any theoretical or experimental performance prediction. Evaluation and prediction of the performance of biometrics systems to identify individuals is important in real-world applications. Researchers have built mathematical models to evaluate and predict the performance of biometrics such as face, fingerprint, iris and gait. Wang and Bhanu. [96, 97] develop a binomial model and a two-dimensional model to predict fingerprint recognition performance. Tan et al. [98] present a two-point model and a three-point model to estimate the error rate for the minutiae based fingerprint recognition. Pankanti et al. [99] address the individuality of fingerprint by estimating the probability of a false correspondence between minutiae based representations from two arbitrary fingerprints belonging to different fingers. Johnson et al. [100] build a CMC model that is based on the feature space to predict the gait identification performance. Wayman [101] derives equations for a general biometric identification system. Daugman [102] analyzes the statistical variability of iris recognition using a binomial model. Johnson et al. [103] model a CMC curve to estimate recognition performance on larger galleries. Grother et al. [104] introduce the joint density function of the match and non-match scores to predict open- and closed-set identification performance.

In this chapter, a binomial model is presented to predict the ear recognition performance. As described in Chapter 4 and Chapter 5, we calculate the RMS registration errors between 3D ears in the probe set with 3D ears in the gallery. RMS errors are used as matching distances to estimate the distribution of match and non-match distances. The *cumulative match characteristic* (CMC) curve is modeled by a binomial distribution and the probability that the match score is within rank r is calculated. Using this model we predict ear recognition performance for a large gallery.

7.2 Performance Prediction

The mathematical prediction model is based on the distribution of match and non-match scores [97, 105]. Let $ms(x)$ and $ns(x)$ denote the distributions of match and non-match scores, in which the match score is the score computed from the true-matched pair and the non-match score is the score computed from the false-matched pair. If the match score is higher, the match is closer. The error occurs when any given match score is less than any of the non-match scores. The probability that the non-match score is greater than or equal to the match score x is $NS(x)$. It is given by equation (7.1)

$$NS(x) = \int_x^\infty ns(t)dt. \tag{7.1}$$

The probability that the match score x has rank r exactly , is given by the binomial probability distribution,

$$C_{r-1}^{N-1}(1 - NS(x))^{N-r}NS(x)^{r-1}. \tag{7.2}$$

By integrating over all the match scores, we get

$$\int_{-\infty}^{\infty} C_{r-1}^{N-1}(1 - NS(x))^{N-r} NS(x)^{r-1} ms(x) dx \qquad (7.3)$$

In theory the match scores can be any value within $(-\infty, \infty)$. Therefore, the probability that the match score is within rank r, which is the definition of a cumulative match characteristic (CMC) curve, is

$$P(N, r) = \sum_{i=1}^{r} \int_{-\infty}^{\infty} C_{i-1}^{N-1}(1 - NS(x))^{N-i} NS(x)^{i-1} ms(x) dx.$$

$$(7.4)$$

In the above equations N is the size of large population whose recognition performance needs to be estimated. Here we assume that the match score and non-match score are independent. Further the match and non-match score distributions for different size galleries are similar. The small size gallery is used to estimate distributions of $ms(x)$ and $ns(x)$. For the ear recognition case, every 3D ear in the probe set is matched to every 3D ear in the gallery set and the RMS registration error is calculated using the procedure described in Section 4.2. This RMS registration error is used as the match criterion.

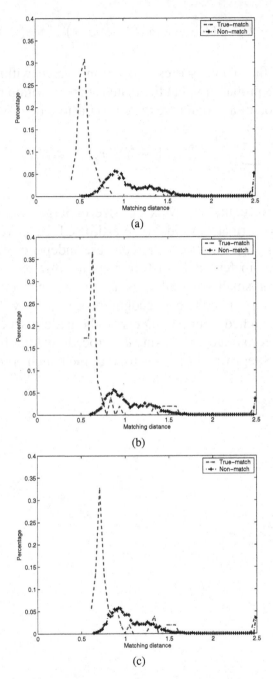

Fig. 7.1. Matching distance distribution for match and non-match pairs for three probe sets: (a) without added noise, (b) with Gaussian noise $N(0, \sigma = 0.6\text{mm})$, (c) with Gaussian noise $N(0, \sigma = 1.0\text{mm})$.

Table 7.1. Predicted and calculated CMC values for three probe sets on 52 subjects. '**P**' denotes 'predicted' and '**C**' denotes 'calculated'.

Probe set	Rank-1		Rank-2		Rank-3	
	P	**C**	**P**	**C**	**P**	**C**
No added noise	92.5%	90.4%	94.6%	96.2%	95.7%	96.2%
$N(0, \sigma = 0.6mm)$	80.4%	76.9%	83.9%	86.5%	85.8%	86.5%
$N(0, \sigma = 1.0mm)$	51.5%	44.2%	60.2%	61.5%	66.1%	67.3%

Table 7.2. Predicted CMC values for three probe sets of larger galleries. The recognition rate is shown as percentage value for the top three ranks (R-1 to R-3).

Probe	N=100			N=200			N=300			N=400		
	R-1	R-2	R-3	R-1	R-2	R-3	R-1	R-2	R-3	R-1	R-2	R-3
Set 1	91.2	92.8	94.4	90.5	90.9	91.8	90.4	90.5	90.8	90.4	90.4	90.5
Set 2	78.3	80.9	83.6	77.1	77.9	79.3	76.9	77.1	77.6	76.9	76.9	77.1
Set 3	46.8	52.1	57.9	44.6	45.9	48.6	44.3	44.6	45.4	44.2	44.3	44.5

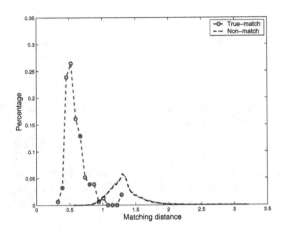

Fig. 7.2. Matching distance distribution for match and non-match pairs on the UCR dataset ES_1.

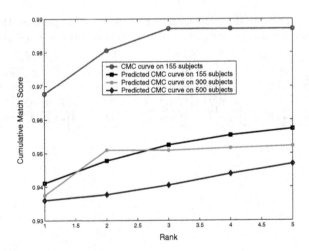

Fig. 7.3. Real and predicted CMC curves on the UCR dataset ES_1.

7.3 Experimental Results

While we were investigating the performance perdiction for 3D ear biometrics, we had a dataset of 52 subjects with 52-pair images. Later, we collected the data on 155 subjects in the UCR dataset. Therefore, we also perform experiments on 155 subjects with 155-pair frontal ears.

7.3.1 Performance Prediction on 52 Pair Images

To predict system's performance in the presence of noise, we inject Gaussian noise to the probe scans along the viewing direction (Z-axis) as described in Section 5.1.5. Given a probe image, we inject Gaussian noise with $\sigma = 0.6$mm and $\sigma = 1.0$mm. Therefore, we have three probe sets: one probe set has no added Gaussian noise; the second probe set has Gaussian noise $N(0, \sigma = 0.6$mm$)$; the third probe set has Gaussian noise $N(0, \sigma = 1.0$mm$)$. Examples of a range image corrupted with Gaussian noise are shown in Figure 5.9.

In the three probe sets, every 3D scan in the three probe sets is matched to every 3D ear in the gallery and the RMS registration error is calculated using the procedure described in Section 4.2. The RMS registration error is used as the matching distance. Therefore, we obtain 52 true-match distances and 1326 (C_2^{52}) non-match distances for every probe set. The matching distance distribution for true-match and non-match for the three probe sets are shown in Figure 7.1. Based on the distributions, we can predict CMC curve $P(N, r)$ where $r = 1, 2, 3$ and N is 52. We also calculate the CMC curve based on the experimental results for three probe sets. The results of the directly calculated CMC curve and the predicted CMC curve are shown in Table 7.1. This table shows that the predicted CMC values are close to the calculated CMC values, which demonstrates the effectiveness of our prediction model. We also predict CMC values for larger galleries from the original range image database of 52 subjects. Table 7.2 shows the predicted CMC values for three probe sets for different gallery size ($N = 100, 200, 300, 400$).

7.3.2 Performance Prediction on 155 Pair Images

We also predict the CMC performance based on the matching distance distributions obtained on the UCR dataset ES_1 using the ear helix and anti-helix representation. Every 3D ear image in the probe set is matched to every 3D ear in the gallery set and the RMS registration error is used as the matching distance. Therefore, 155 true-match distances and 11,935 (C_2^{155}) non-match distances are obtained. The matching distance distributions for the true-match and the non-match are shown in Figure 7.2. Note that there is an overlap between the two distributions, which accounts for false matches. Based on the distributions, the CMC curve $P(N, r)$ can be predicted where $r = 1, 2, 3, 4, 5$ and N is the database size. The results of the directly calculated CMC curve and the predicted CMC curve are shown in Figure 7.3. Figure 7.3 shows that the predicted CMC values on 155 subjects are close to the real CMC values, which demonstrates the effectiveness of the prediction model. The predicted CMC curves for larger datasets of 300 and 500 subjects are also provided in Figure 7.3 which shows that the recognition performance degrades slowly with the increase in database size. This suggests the scalability of the proposed recognition system.

7.4 Conclusions

In this chapter, we predict the ear recognition performance on larger galleries by modeling cumulative match characteristic curve as a binomial distribution. Table 7.2 and Figure 7.3 demonstrate that we can predict the recognition performance for lager galleries. The performance prediction model shows that the proposed ear recognition system is scalable with the increased database size.

Applications of the Proposed Techniques

The techniques we proposed in Chapter 3 and Chapter 5 are general techniques in computer vision and pattern recognition. For example, the local surface patch (LSP) representation can be used to recognize 3D general objects; the global-to-local registration with the optimization framework can handle non-rigid shape registration. We discuss the applications of these two techniques in this chapter with several non-ear examples.

8.1 LSP Representation for General 3D Object Recognition

The LSP representation introduced in Chapter 5 for ear recognition is a general surface descriptor applicable to any 3D objects. In this subchapter, we propose a general 3D object recognition system using the LSP representation. In order to speed up the retrieval of surface descriptors and to deal with a large set of objects, the local surface patches of models are indexed into a hash table. Given a set of test local surface patches, votes are cast for models containing similar surface descriptors. Based on the votes for potential corresponding local surface patches the candidate models are hypothesized. The verification is performed by aligning models with the test data for the most likely models that occurs in a scene.

8.1.1 Local Surface Patch

Similar to the LSP representation introduced in Chapter 5, the surface type T_p of a LSP is obtained based on the Gaussian and mean curvatures of a feature point using equation (8.1) where H is the mean curvature and K is the Gaussian curvature [106, 107]. There are eight surface types determined by the signs of Gaussian and mean curvatures given in Table 8.1. A local surface patch is shown in Figure 8.1.

$$Tp = 1 + 3(1 + sgn_{\epsilon_H}(H)) + (1 - sgn_{\epsilon_K}(K))$$

$$sgn_{\epsilon_x}(X) = \begin{cases} +1 \; if \;\; X > \epsilon_x \\ 0 \;\;\; if \;\; |X| \leq \epsilon_x \\ -1 \; if \;\; X < \epsilon_x \end{cases} \qquad (8.1)$$

In this chapter, feature points are defined in areas with large shape variations as measured by the shape index values calculated from the principal curvatures. The shape index values are calculated as described in Section 5.1.

Figure 8.2 shows the range image of an object and its shape index image. In Figure 8.2(a), the darker pixels are away from the camera while the lighter ones are closer. In Figure 8.2(b), the brighter points denote large shape index values which correspond to ridge and dome surfaces while the darker pixels denote small shape index values which correspond to valley and cup surfaces. From Figure 8.2, we can see that shape index values can capture the characteristics of the shape of objects, which suggests that shape index can be used for extraction of feature points. In other words, the center point is marked as a feature point if its shape index S_i satisfies equation (8.2) within a $w \times w$ window placed at a pixel in an image.

$$S_i = \text{max of shape indexes and } S_i \geq (1 + \alpha) * \mu$$
$$\text{or } S_i = \text{min of shape indexes and } S_i \leq (1 - \beta) * \mu$$

$$\text{where } \mu = \frac{1}{M} \sum_{j=1}^{M} S_i(j) \quad 0 \leq \alpha, \beta \leq 1. \qquad (8.2)$$

In equation (8.2) α, β parameters control the selection of feature points and M is the number of points in the local window. The results of feature extraction are shown in Figure 8.3 where the feature points are marked by red dots. From Figure 8.3, we can clearly see that some feature points corresponding to the same physical area appear in both images.

Table 8.1. Surface type Tp based on the signs of Mean curvature (H) and Gaussian curvature (K).

Mean Curvature H	$K > 0$	$K = 0$	$K < 0$
$H < 0$	Peak $T_p = 1$	Ridge $T_p = 2$	Saddle Ridge $T_p = 3$
$H = 0$	None $T_p = 4$	Flat $T_p = 5$	Minimal $T_p = 6$
$H > 0$	Pit $T_p = 7$	Valley $T_p = 8$	Saddle Valley $T_p = 9$

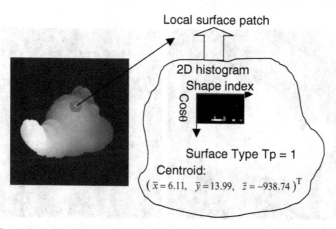

Local surface patch

2D histogram
Shape index

$\cos\theta$

Surface Type Tp = 1
Centroid:
$(\bar{x} = 6.11, \quad \bar{y} = 13.99, \quad \bar{z} = -938.74)^{\mathrm{T}}$

Fig. 8.1. Illustration of a local surface patch (LSP). Feature point P is marked by the asterisk and its neighbors N are marked by the dots. The surface type of the LSP is 1 based on Table 8.1.

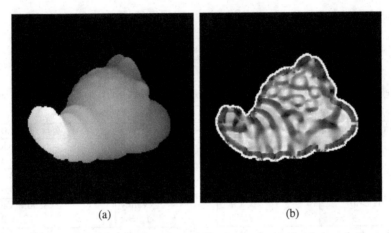

(a)   (b)

Fig. 8.2. (a) A range image and (b) its shape index image. In (a), the darker pixels are away from the camera and the lighter ones are closer. In (b), the darker pixels correspond to concave surfaces and the lighter ones correspond to convex surfaces.

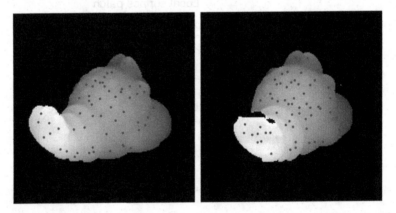

Fig. 8.3. Feature points location (·) in two range images, shown as gray scale images, of the same object taken at different viewpoints.

8.1.2 Hash Table Building

Considering the uncertainty of location of a feature point, we also calculate descriptors of local surface patches for neighbors of a feature point P. To speed up the retrieval of local surface patches, for each LSP we compute the mean ($\mu = \frac{1}{L}\sum_{l=1}^{L} S_i(p_l)$) and standard deviation ($\sigma^2 = \frac{1}{L-1}\sum_{l=1}^{L}(S_i(p_l) - \mu)^2$) of the shape index values in a neighborhood around the feature point where L is the number of points on the LSP under consideration such that the angle between the surface normal at the feature point and its neighboring points is small. p_l is the lth point on the LSP. We use LSPs to index a hash table and insert into the corresponding hash bin the information about the model LSPs. Thus, the model local surface descriptors are saved into the hash table. For each model object, we repeat the same process to build the model database. The structure of the hash table is explained in Figure 8.4, where every bin in the hash table has an associated linked list which saves the information of the model surface descriptors in terms of model ID, 2D histogram, surface type and the centroid; and the accumulator keeps track of the number of votes that each model receives.

8.1.3 Hypotheses Generation

Given a test range image, we extract feature points and get local surface patches. Then we calculate the mean and stand deviation of shape index, and cast votes to the hash table if the histogram dissimilarity falls below a preset threshold ϵ_2 and the surface type is the same. The dissimilarity between the two histograms is evaluated by equation (5.3).

After voting, we histogram all hash table entries and get models which received the top three highest votes. By casting votes, we not only know which models get higher votes, but also we know the potential corresponding local surface patch pairs. Note that a hash table entry may have multiple items, we choose the local surface patch from the database with minimum dissimilarity and the same surface type as the possible corresponding patch. We filter the possible corresponding pairs based on the geometric constraints (5.4). Figure 8.5 shows one example of partitioning corresponding pairs into groups. It shows the grouping results for an object imaged at two different viewpoints. Figure 8.5(a) shows the feature point extraction result for the test object.

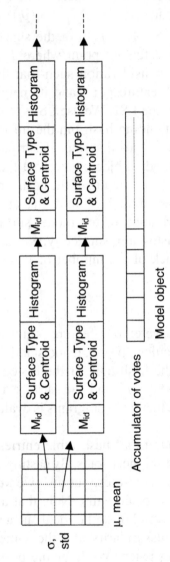

Fig. 8.4. Structure of the hash table. Every entry in the hash table has a linked list which saves information about the model LSPs and the accumulator records the number of votes that each model receives.

Comparing the local surface patches with LSPs on the model object and casting votes to the hash table, the initial corresponding LSP pairs are shown in Figure 8.5(b), in which every pair is represented by the same number superimposed on the test and model images. We observe that both the true and false corresponding pairs are found. After applying the simple geometric constraint (5.4), the filtered largest group is shown in Figure 8.5(c), in which the pairs satisfying the constraint (5.4) are put into one group. We observe that true correspondences between the model and the test objects are obtained by comparing local surface patches, casting votes to the hash table and using the simple geometric constraint.

8.1.4 Verification

Given the corresponding LSPs between a model-test pair, the initial rigid transformation, which brings the model and test objects into a coarse alignment, can be estimated by minimizing the sum of the squares of theses errors ($\Sigma = \frac{1}{n} \sum_{l=1}^{n} |S_l - R*M_l - T|^2$) with respect to the rotation matrix R and the translation vector T. The rotation matrix and translation vector are computed by using the quaternion representation [76].

Given the estimate of initial rigid transformation, the purpose of iterative closest point (ICP) algorithm [63] is to determine if the match is good and to find a refined alignment between them. If the probe ear is really an instance of the gallery ear, the ICP algorithm will result in a good registration and a large number of corresponding points between gallery and probe ear surfaces will be found. Since ICP algorithm requires that the test data set is a subset of the model set, we use the modified ICP algorithm proposed by Zhang [70] to remove outliers based on the distance distribution.

Starting with the initial transformation obtained from the coarse alignment, the modified ICP algorithm is run to refine the transformation by minimizing the distance between the control points of the model object and their closest points of the test objecct. For each object in the model database, the control points are randomly selected and the modified ICP is applied to those points. We repeat the same procedure 15 times and choose the rigid transformation with the minimum root mean square (RMS) error. The object in the model database with the minimum RMS error is declared as the recognized object. In the

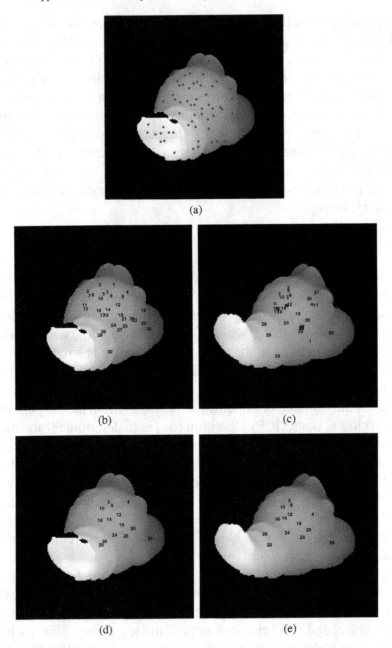

Fig. 8.5. An example of corresponding LSPs. (a) Feature points marked as dots on the test object. (b) Test object with matched LSPs after hashing. (c) A model object with matched LSPs after hashing. (d) Test object in Figure 8.5(b) with matched LSPs after applying the geometric constraint (5.4). (e) The model object in Figure 8.5(c) with matched LSPs after applying the geometric constraint (5.4).

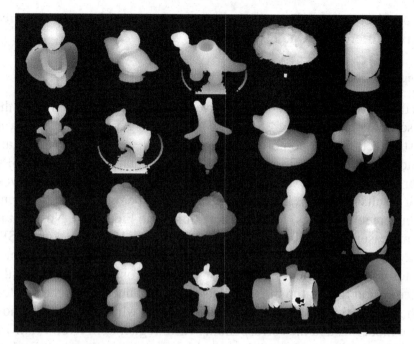

Fig. 8.6. The range images of objects in the model database. The object IDs (0 to 19) are labeled from left to right and top to bottom.

modified ICP algorithm, the speed bottleneck is the nearest neighbor search. Therefore, the kd-tree structure is used in the implementation.

8.1.5 Experimental Results

Data and Parameters

We use real range data collected by Ohio State University.[1] There are 20 objects in our database and the range image of the model objects are shown in Figure 8.6. The parameters of our approach are $\epsilon_1 = 6.5$mm, $A = \pi/3$, $\epsilon_2 = 0.75$, $\epsilon_3 = 9.4$mm, $\alpha = 0.35$, $\beta = 0.2$, and $\epsilon_H = \epsilon_K = 0.003$. Note that A, ϵ_1, ϵ_3 parameters are the same as in Chapter 5. The new parameters in this chapter are ϵ_2, ϵ_H, ϵ_K, α and β. The number of bins in the shape index axis is 17 and the number of bins in the other axis (cos θ) is 34. The total number of LSPs calculated in the model objects is about 34,000. The average size of local surface patch is 230 pixels. We apply our approach to the single-object and

---

[1] http://sampl.eng.ohio-state.edu/sampl/data/3DDB/RID/minolta/

two-object scenes. The model objects and scene objects are captured at two different viewpoints.

Single-Object Scenes

In this test case, we show the effectiveness of the voting scheme and the discriminating power of LSP in the hypothesis generation. For a given test object, feature points are extracted and the properties of LSPs are calculated. Then LSPs are indexed into the database of model LSPs. For each model indexed, its vote is increased by one. We show the voting results (shown as a percentage of the number of LSPs in the scene which received votes) for the twenty objects in Figure 8.7. Note that in some cases the numbers shown are larger than 100 since some LSPs may receive more than one vote. We observe that most of the highest votes go to the correct models. For every test object, we perform the verification for the top three models which obtained the highest votes. The verification results are listed in Table 8.2, which shows the candidate model ID and the corresponding RMS registration error. From Table 8.2, we observe that all the test objects are correctly recognized. In order to examine the recognition results visually, we display the model object and test object in the same image before and after the alignment for four examples. The images in Figure 8.8 (top figure) show test objects and their corresponding model objects before alignment. The images in Figure 8.8 (bottom figure) show test objects and the correctly recognized model objects after alignment. We observe that each model object is well aligned with the corresponding test object and the test cases with large pose variations (up to $45°$) are correctly handled. Since the proposed LSP representation consists of histogram of shape index and surface normal angle, they are invariant to rigid transformation. The experimental results verified the view-point invariance of the LSP representation.

Two-Object Scenes

We created four two-object scenes to make one object partially overlap the other object as follows. We first properly translated objects along the x and y axes, and then resampled the surface to create a range image. The visible points on the surface were identified using the Z-buffer algorithm. Table 8.3 provides the objects included in the four

	0	1	2	3	4	5	6	7	8	9	10	11	12	13	14	15	16	17	18	19
0	**69**	16	69	27	36	11	40	7	33	24	49	60	33	7	20	16	4	0	51	49
1	51	116	75	44	46	30	42	40	104	53	100	**118**	79	32	38	2	67	14	65	79
2	63	56	**146**	54	61	8	76	41	78	54	82	76	49	45	39	8	52	2	53	63
3	21	21	60	**76**	44	7	44	39	55	10	55	63	71	31	18	10	31	0	10	50
4	35	44	30	25	**69**	5	12	17	67	37	67	50	19	28	7	5	25	0	35	51
5	8	20	11	5	2	**120**	5	22	5	5	31	25	17	0	0	0	25	54	5	5
6	68	49	158	52	30	6	**171**	53	76	57	73	83	78	42	39	19	45	0	105	46
7	10	62	12	20	12	55	27	**102**	60	12	82	55	57	15	0	15	40	62	30	65
8	50	61	86	53	50	26	45	36	**172**	58	113	94	93	28	24	30	57	12	65	87
9	30	32	48	13	36	3	55	3	86	**92**	26	44	32	30	17	40	46	0	63	28
10	43	85	68	80	61	48	58	81	118	38	**143**	114	75	21	31	13	68	8	85	123
11	18	86	68	47	38	33	83	76	63	29	80	**104**	90	45	40	6	63	7	63	100
12	57	72	75	79	62	22	90	88	75	31	87	127	**131**	79	24	14	61	9	61	100
13	31	75	68	27	44	10	41	27	58	27	51	65	41	**79**	6	3	51	0	27	44
14	31	51	100	37	72	6	72	17	**106**	41	89	93	51	65	96	6	48	0	55	86
15	5	65	10	5	0	25	0	15	35	15	35	25	25	10	0	**110**	60	20	25	10
16	35	64	69	41	58	19	48	42	**105**	42	83	85	42	39	21	8	103	10	37	58
17	5	43	7	0	2	53	0	25	17	7	41	43	23	7	0	2	30	**87**	0	10
18	9	30	44	11	13	13	50	21	63	26	67	59	48	26	11	13	25	0	**161**	55
19	40	49	63	44	32	7	51	47	105	43	108	87	57	47	36	18	30	2	64	**115**

Fig. 8.7. Voting results, shown as a percentage of the number of LSPs in the scene which received votes, for twenty models in the single-object scenes. Each row shows the voting results of a test object to 20 model objects. The maximum vote in each row is bounded by a box.

Table 8.2. Verification results for single-object scenes. The first number in the parenthesis is the model object ID and the second one is the RMS registration error. The unit of registration error is in millimeters (mm).

Test objects	Results (Top 3 matches)		
0	**(0, 0.624)**	(2, 4.724)	(11, 1.529)
1	(11, 3.028)	**(1, 0.314)**	(8, 3.049)
2	**(2, 0.504)**	(10, 2.322)	(8, 2.148)
3	**(3, 0.913)**	(12, 2.097)	(11, 1.335)
4	**(4, 0.632)**	(8, 2.372)	(10, 1.781)
5	**(5, 0.217)**	(17, 2.081)	(10, 3.146)
6	**(6, 0.5632)**	(2, 3.840)	(18, 4.692)
7	**(7, 0.214)**	(10, 2.835)	(19, 3.901)
8	**(8, 0.426)**	(10, 1.326)	(11, 2.691)
9	**(9, 0.459)**	(8, 2.639)	(18, 4.745)
10	**(10, 0.263)**	(19, 2.451)	(8, 3.997)
11	**(11, 0.373)**	(19, 3.773)	(12, 1.664)
12	**(12, 0.525)**	(11, 1.698)	(19, 4.149)
13	**(13, 0.481)**	(1, 1.618)	(2, 4.378)
14	(8, 2.694)	(2, 4.933)	**(14, 0.731)**
15	**(15, 0.236)**	(1, 2.849)	(16, 4.919)
16	(8, 3.586)	**(16, 0.306)**	(11, 1.499)
17	**(17, 0.252)**	(5, 2.033)	(11, 2.494)
18	**(18, 0.395)**	(10, 2.316)	(8, 2.698)
19	**(19, 0.732)**	(10, 2.948)	(8, 3.848)

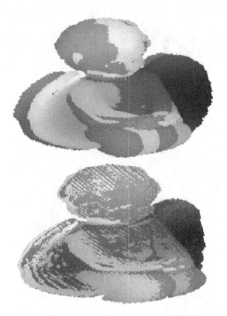

Fig. 8.8. Four examples of correctly recognized model-test pairs. Each row shows one example. The test objects are shaded light gray while the recognized model objects are shaded dark gray and overlaid on the test objects. The top figure shows the model and test objects before alignment, and the bottom one shows the model and test objects after alignment. For the range images of model objects, the lighter pixels are closer to the camera and the darker pixels are away from the camera. In example 1 shown here, the rotation angle is $20.4°$ and the axis is $[0.0319, 0.9670, 0.2526]^T$.

Fig. 8.8. Figure 8.8 Continued, Example 2. The rotation angle is $35.9°$ and the axis is $[-0.0304, -0.5714, -0.1660]^T$.

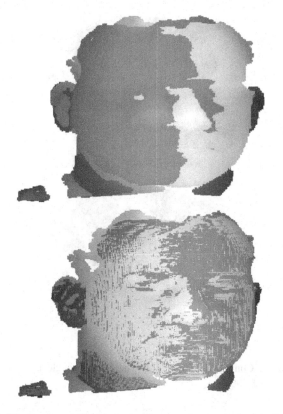

Fig. 8.8. Figure 8.8 Continued, Example 3. The rotation angle is 14.1° and the axis is $[0.0187, 0.2429, 0.0046]^T$.

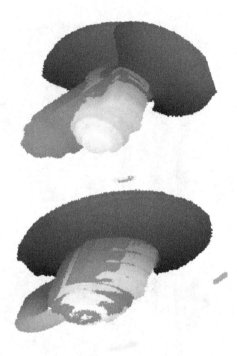

Fig. 8.8. Figure 8.8 Continued, Example 4. The rotation angle is $43.6°$ and the axis is $[0.6855, -0.6150, -1.3909]^T$.

Table 8.3. Voting and registration results for the four two-object scenes shown in Figure 8.9(a). The first number in the parenthesis is the model object ID, the second one is the voting result and the third one is RMS registration error. The unit of registration error is in millimeters (mm).

Test	Objects in the image	Voting and registration results for top 6 matches					
Scene 0	1, 10	**(10, 137, 0.69)**	**(1, 109, 0.35)**	(11, 109, 1.86)	(2, 102, 5.00)	(12, 100, 1.78)	(19, 98, 2.14)
Scnee 1	13, 16	(11, 72, 2.51)	(8, 56, 2.69)	(2, 56, 3.67)	**(13, 56, 0.50)**	(10, 51, 1.98)	**(16, 48, 0.53)**
Scene 2	6, 9	**(6, 129, 1.31)**	(2, 119, 3.31)	(18, 79, 3.74)	(8, 76, 2.99)	**(9, 56, 0.55)**	(12, 52, 1.97)
Scene 3	4, 12	**(4, 113, 0.81)**	(8, 113, 2.09)	(11, 88, 1.69)	(2, 86, 3.05)	(10, 81, 1.89)	(19, 74, 3.85)

Fig. 8.9. Recognition results for the four two-object scenes. Example 1 is shown here. The test objects are shaded light gray while the recognized model objects are shaded dark gray. The top figure shows the range images of the four two-object scenes, and the bottom one shows the recognized model objects overlaid on the test objects with the recovered pose. For the range images of model objects, the lighter pixels are closer to the camera and the darker pixels are away from the camera. Note that in Example 4 one object is missed.

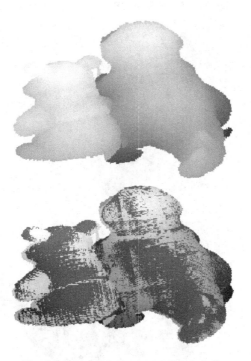

Fig. 8.9. Figure 8.9 Continued, Example 2.

Fig. 8.9. Figure 8.9 Continued, Example 3.

Fig. 8.9. Figure 8.9 Continued, Example 4.

scens and the voting and registration results for the top six candidate model objects. The candidate models are ordered according to the percentage of votes they received and each candidate model is verified by the ICP algorithm. We observe that the objects in the first three scenes objects are correctly recognized and the object 12 is missed in the fourth scene since the vote it obtained was not ranked on the top. The four scenes are shown in Figure 8.9 (top figure). The recognition results are shown in Figure 8.9 (bottom figure). We observe that the recognized model objects are well aligned with the corresponding test objects.

8.1.6 Comparison with the Spin Image and the Spherical Spin Image Representations

We compared the distinctive power of the LSP representation with the spin image (SI) [3] and the spherical spin image (SSI) [4] representations. We conducted the following experiments. We take 20 model objects, compute feature points as described in Section 8.1.1 and calculate the surface descriptors at those feature points and their neighbors. Given a test object, we calculate the surface descriptors for the extracted feature points, find their nearest neighbors, apply the geometric constraint and perform the verification by comparing it against all the model objects. In the experiments, both of the size of the spin image and the spherical spin image are 15×15. We achieved 100% recognition rate by the three representations. However, the average computation time for the three representations are different. The total time (T) for recognizing a single object consists of three timings:

- find the nearest neighbors t_a;
- find the group of corresponding surface descriptors t_b;
- perform the verification t_c.

These timings, on a Linux machine with an *AMD Opteron* 1.8 GHz processor, are listed in Table 8.4. We observe that the LSP representation runs the fastest for searching the nearest neighbors because the LSPs are formed based on the surface type and the comparison of LSPs is based on the surface type and the histogram dissimilarity.

8.1.7 Discussions

From the experimental results, we observe that the integrated local surface descriptor (LSP) is really effective for surface representation and

Table 8.4. The timing in seconds for the three representations. LSP denotes the local surface patch descriptor; SI denotes the spin image [3]; SSI denotes the spherical spin image [4].

	t_a	t_b	t_c	$\mathcal{T}$
LSP	21.46	0.8	67.16	89.42
SI	95.26	0.67	66.14	162.07
SSI	83.63	0.66	66.28	150.57

3D object recognition. For fast retrieval of surface descriptors, the generated LSPs for all models are indexed into a hash table. During recognition, surface descriptors computed for the scene are used to index the hash table, casting the votes for the models which contain the similar surface descriptors. The candidate models are ordered according to the number of votes received by the models. Verification is performed by aligning models with scenes for the most likely models. Experimental results on the real range data have shown the validity and effectiveness of the proposed approach: geometric hashing scheme for fast retrieval of surface descriptors and comparison of LSPs for the establishment of correspondences. Comparison with the spin image and spherical spin image representations shows that our representation is as effective for the matching of 3D objects as these two representations but it is efficient by a factor of 3.89 (over SSI) to 4.37 (over SI) for finding corresponding parts between a model-test pair. This is because the LSPs are formed based on the surface type and the comparison of LSPs is based on the surface type and the histogram dissimilarity.

8.2 Global-to-Local Non-Rigid Shape Registration

Registration of non-rigid shapes is an important issue in computer vision and it has drawn an increasing attention due to its wide range of applications related to recognition, tracking and retrieval. The shape registration problem can be stated as follows: Given two shapes, a model shape M and a target shape S, find the best transformation that assigns any point of M a corresponding point in S and minimizes the dissimilarity between the transformed shape $\hat{M}$ and S. Therefore, there are two problems to be resolved: the correspondence, and the transformation.

The non-rigid shape registration is much harder since it has more degrees of freedom than the rigid shape registration problem. Recently researchers have come up with different approaches to solve the non-rigid shape registration problem [72, 108–111]. Chui and Rangarajan [72] presented an optimization based approach, TPS-RPM (thin plate spline-robust point matching) algorithm, to jointly estimate the correspondence and non-rigid transformations between two point-based shapes. Belongie et al. [108] proposed a descriptor called *shape context* to find correspondences by minimizing the overall shape context distances and the TPS transformation is iteratively solved. Guo et al. [109] described a joint clustering and diffeomorphism estimation algorithm that can simultaneously estimate the correspondence and fit the diffeomorphism between the two point sets (a diffeomorphism is a invertible function that maps one differentiable manifold to another such that both the function and its inverse are smooth). Paragios et al. [110] introduced a simple and robust shape representation (distance functions) and a variational framework for global-to-local registration in which a linear motion model and a local deformation field are incrementally recovered. Zheng and Doermann [111] presented a relaxation labeling based point matching algorithm for aligning non-rigid shapes. The point matching is formulated as a graph matching problem to preserve local neighborhood structures in which the point is a node and neighboring points are connected by edges.

As compared to these approaches, we decompose the non-rigid shape registration into a two-step procedure:

- the global similarity transformation that brings the model shape and target shape into a coarse alignment;
- the local deformation that deforms the transformed model shape to the target shape [112].

For the first step, feature based registration is employed; in the second step the local deformation is formulated as an optimization problem to preserve the structure of the shape model.

8.2.1 Global Similarity Registration

The task of the global registration is to find a similarity transformation between M and S that includes three parameters (s, θ, T); a scale factor s, a rotation θ and a translation vector $T = (T_x, T_y)$.

$$S = s \begin{bmatrix} \cos\theta & \sin\theta \\ -\sin\theta & \cos\theta \end{bmatrix} M + \begin{bmatrix} T_x \\ T_y \end{bmatrix} \qquad (8.3)$$

Once the corresponding pairs (M_i, S_i) are known, the three parameters can be estimated by minimizing the sum of square distance between the transformed M_i and S_i.

The shape context descriptor [108] is used to find the correspondence only. Considering the shape contexts of two point a and b, the cost C_{ab} of matching the two points is evaluated by χ^2 test statistic since shape contexts are histograms that can approximate probability distributions.

$$C_{ab} = C(a,b) = \frac{1}{2} \sum_{i=1}^{K} \frac{(h_a(i) - h_b(i))^2}{h_a(i) + h_b(i)} \qquad (8.4)$$

where $h_a(i)$ and $h_b(i)$ denote the K-bin normalized histograms at points a and b respectively. Given the sets of costs $C(a, b)$ between pairs a on the model shape and b on the target shape, the optimal correspondence is found by minimizing the sum of individual matching costs. This is solved by a bipartite matching algorithm with the one-to-one matching constraint [108]. In our case, the configuration of the model shape is fixed and we resample the points from the contour of the model shape. Then we compute shape context descriptors to find the correspondences of the model shape in the target shape to calculate the global similarity transformation, while in [108] the non-linear TPS transformation is solved iteratively by warping the model shape to the target and recovering correspondences. Figure 8.10 shows one example of the global similarity registration result; Figure 8.10 shows the model shape and the target shape before alignment; Figure 8.10 (a) shows the transformed model shape is superimposed on the target shape after alignment. The three parameters are $s = 1.28, \theta = 45.3°, T = (-36.4, 77.9)$ pixels. We observe that the model shape is roughly aligned with the target shape.

8.2.2 Local Deformation

After the model shape is brought into coarse alignment with the target shape through the global registration, it needs to deform to the target

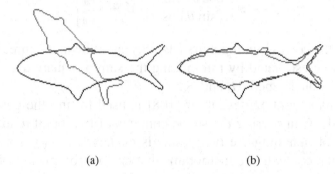

(a)   (b)

Fig. 8.10. Global similarity registration. The model shape is shown in red and the target shape is shown in black). (a) Initial condition. (b) Global similarity registration result.

shape with the structure of the shape model preserved. The local deformation is model by the thin plate spline (TPS) transformation that is widely used in shape matching. As described in Section 3.2.3, we can achieve this task by minimizing the proposed cost function,

$$E(\mathbf{x}, \mathbf{y}) = E_{img}(\mathbf{x}, \mathbf{y}) + \gamma E_D(\mathbf{x}, \mathbf{y})$$

$$= \sum_{i=1}^{n} g(|\nabla I_m(x_i, y_i)|) + \frac{1}{2}\gamma(\mathbf{x}^T K \mathbf{x} + \mathbf{y}^T K \mathbf{y}). \quad (8.5)$$

As derived in Chapter 3.2.3, the coordinates of $(\mathbf{x}, \mathbf{y})$ can be iteratively updated by

$$\mathbf{x}_t = (\gamma K + \alpha I)^{-1}\Big(\alpha \mathbf{x}_{t-1} +$$

$$\sum_{i=1}^{n} \frac{1}{(1 + |\nabla I_{step}^{t-1}(x_i, y_i)|)^2} \frac{\partial |\nabla I_{step}^{t-1}(x_i, y_i)|}{\partial \mathbf{x}}\Big)$$

$$\mathbf{y}_t = (\gamma K + \alpha I)^{-1}\Big(\alpha \mathbf{y}_{t-1} +$$

$$\sum_{i=1}^{n} \frac{1}{(1 + |\nabla I_{step}^{t-1}(x_i, y_i)|)^2} \frac{\partial |\nabla I_{step}^{t-1}(x_i, y_i)|}{\partial \mathbf{y}}\Big). \quad (8.6)$$

Figure 8.11 shows an example of deforming the model shape (dude) to the target shape at iteration 0, 25, 50, 75, 100, and 125. We observe that the model shape is brought more closer to the target shape during the deformation.

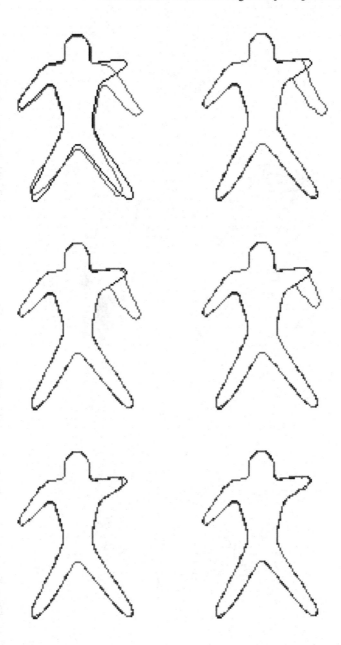

Fig. 8.11. Deformation of the transformed model shape to the target shape at iteration 0, 25, 50, 75, 100, and 125. The model shape is show in red and the target shape is shown in black.

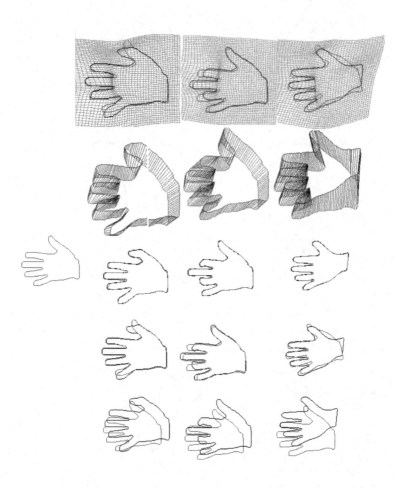

Fig. 8.12. Global-to-local registration results for the shape of hand. The model shape is shown in red and the target shape is shown in black. The first row shows the model shape. The second, third, and fourth rows show examples with different initial conditions. For rows 2–4, the first column shows the initial condition; the second column shows global registration; the third column shows local deformation; the fourth column shows correspondences, and the fifth column shows grid deformation.

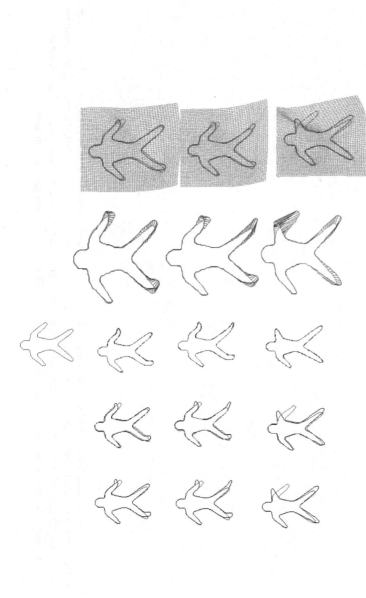

Fig. 8.13. Global-to-local registration results for the shape of dude. The model shape is shown in red and the target shape is shown in black. The first row shows the model shape. The second, third, and fourth rows show examples with different initial conditions. For rows 2–4, the first column shows the initial condition; the second column shows global registration; the third column shows local deformation; the fourth column shows correspondences, and the fifth column shows grid deformation.

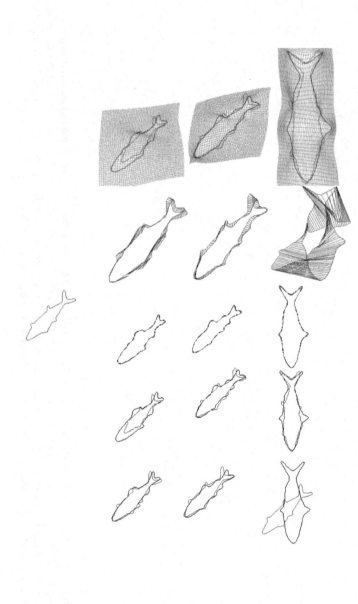

Fig. 8.14. Global-to-local registration results for the shape of fish. The model shape is shown in red and the target shape is shown in black. The first row shows the model shape. The second, third, and fourth rows show examples with different initial conditions. For rows 2–4, the first column shows the initial condition; the second column shows global registration; the third column shows local deformation; the fourth column shows correspondences, and the fifth column shows grid deformation.

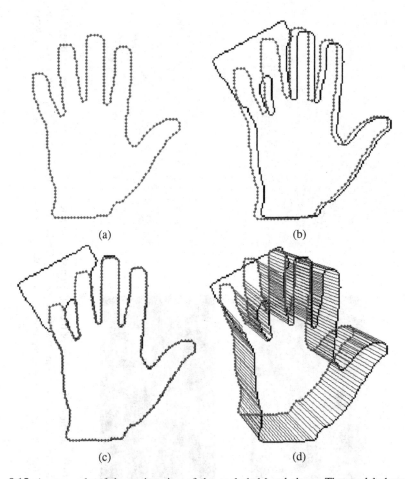

Fig. 8.15. An example of the registration of the occluded hand shape. The model shape is shown with dotted line and the target shape is shown with solid line. (a) Model shape. (b) Global registration. (c) Local deformation driven by the proposed optimization formulation. (d) Correspondences. Note that the target hand shape is occluded.

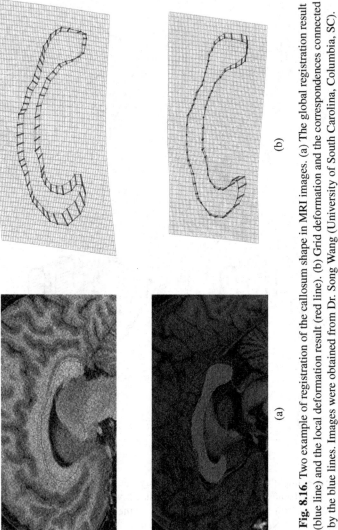

Fig. 8.16. Two example of registration of the callosum shape in MRI images. (a) The global registration result (blue line) and the local deformation result (red line). (b) Grid deformation and the correspondences connected by the blue lines. Images were obtained from Dr. Song Wang (University of South Carolina, Columbia, SC).

8.2.3 Experimental Results on Binary Images

We used the shape database collected by Brown University.[2] Figures 8.12, 8.13 and 8.14 show the non-rigid shape global-to-local registration results on three shapes of the hand, dude, and fish, respectively. The regularization term γ for shapes of the hand, dude and fish is 20, 100, 25, respectively. In the three figures, the first row shows the model shape and the columns below the model shape show the model shape and target shape before the global registration, the transformed model shape overlaid on the target shape after the global alignment, the registration results after local shape deformation, the one-to-one correspondence connected by the blue lines, and the warped regular grids by the local deformation computed from equation (3.18). From Figures 8.12, 8.13 and 8.14, we see that the model shape is successfully deformed to the target shape and the one-to-one correspondence is established.

Figure 8.15 shows the registration of the model shape with the occluded target shape. Since the shape model encodes the prior information about the shape topology, the registration of the occluded shape can be handled. We observe that the model shape is driven towards the target shape by the optimization formulation.

Quantitative evaluation: The accuracy of the proposed approach is quantified by the average Euclidean distance between the points in the transformed model shape and the correspondences in the target shape. The average distances after the local deformation for the shapes of hand, dude and fish are 0.59, 0.45, and 0.61 pixels, respectively; while the distances after global alignment are 1.84, 1.80, and 2.49 pixels. We observe that the proposed global-to-local non-rigid shape registration algorithm brings the model shape and the target shape into a good alignment.

8.2.4 Experimental Results on Gray-Level Images

The proposed formulation is also valid for gray-levle images as well as binary images. Figure 8.16 shows the registration of callosum in a human brain MRI image. Figure 8.16(a) shows the global registration result by the blue line and local deformation result by the red line; Figure 8.16(b) shows the grid deformation in which the correspondences are connected by the blue lines.

---

[2] http://www.lems.brown.edu/vision/

8.2.5 Discussions

We have proposed a novel global-to-local procedure for aligning non-rigid shapes. Since the structure of the model shape should be preserved under the deformation, the bending energy is incorporated into the optimization formulation as a regularization term to penalize the large shape deformation. The optimization procedure drives the initial global registration towards the target shape with the structure of the model shape preserved and finally finds one-to-one correspondence between the model shape and target shape. Experimental results on three non-rigid shapes show the effectiveness of the proposed approach.

8.3 Conclusions

In this chapter, we presented two general applications in the field of computer vision and pattern recognition. First, we presented 3D object recognition results on general 3D range images. We use the local surface patch (LSP) representation that has been used for ear recognition. The only difference in LSP representation used for ears and general 3D objects is the number of surface types. In 3D ear recognition, the surface takes three different types (concave, saddle, and convex). For the general 3D object recognition, the surface takes eight different types (peak, ridge, saddle ridge, flat, minimal, pit, valley, and saddle valley).

We also presented a global-to-local registration scheme for the precise alignment of a variety of images collected from various applications. These images included hand images, dude images, fish images, and MRI images.

9

Summary and Future Work

9.1 Summary

This book has presented a complete human identification system using 3D ear biometrics. The system consists of 3D ear detection, 3D ear identification/verification and performance prediction. In the following, we provide a summary of key ideas that are presented in this book.

- For accurate localization of ear in the side face range images, a single reference 3D shape model is adapted to an image following the global-to-local registration procedure within an optimization framework. The detection starts from the extraction of regions-of-interest (ROIs) by fusion of color and range images. Once ROIs are extracted, the problem of localizing ear is converted to the alignment of the reference 3D shape model with ROIs. The alignment follows a global-to-local registration procedure. The local deformation is performed within an optimization formulation in which the bending energy of thin plate spline is incorporated as a regularization term to preserve the topology of the shape model. The optimization procedure drives the initial global registration closer towards the target. We achieved 99.3% correct detection rate on the UCR dataset and 87.71% on the UND dataset without retuning the parameters of the detection algorithm on different datasets. Furthermore, the optimization formulation is general and can be used to handle non-rigid shape registration.
- After the ear is automatically extracted from the side face range images, we proposed two different representations for surface matching.

The first representation is the ear helix/anti-helix, whose 3D coordinates are obtained from the detection algorithm; the second representation is the local surface patch (LSP) which is invariant to rotation and translation. We used these representations for finding initial correspondences between a gallery-probe pair. Then a modified iterative closest point (ICP) algorithm iteratively refined the transformation which brings the hypothesized gallery and a probe image into the best alignment. The root mean square (RMS) registration error is used as the matching error criterion. The experimental results on two real ear range and color image datasets demonstrated the potential of the proposed algorithms for robust ear recognition in 3D. Extensive experiments are performed on the UCR dataset (155 subjects with 902 images under pose variations), the UND dataset Collection F (302 subjects with 302 time-lapse gallery-probe pairs) and a subset of the UND dataset G for evaluating the performance with respect to pose variations without retuning the parameters of the proposed algorithms. These results showed that the proposed ear recognition system is capable of recognizing ears under pose variations, partial occlusions and time lapse effects. The proposed representations are less sensitive to pose variations. We also provided a comparison of the LSP representation with the spin image representation for identification and verification. This comparison showed that the LSP representation achieved a slightly better performance than the spin image representation.

- For the identification, usually the system conducts a one-to-many comparison to establish an individual's identity. This process is computationally expensive especially for a large database. Therefore, we presented a general framework for rapid recognition of 3D ears which combines the feature embedding and SVM rank learning techniques. Unlike the previous work for fast object recognition in 3D range images, we achieved a sublinear time complexity on the number of models without making any assumptions about the feature distributions. The experimental results on the UCR dataset (155 subjects with 902 ear images) and the UND dataset (302 subjects with 604 ear images) containing 3D ear objects demonstrated the performance and effectiveness of the proposed framework. The average processing time per query are 72 seconds and 192 seconds, respectively, on the two datasets with the reduction by a factor of 6 compared to the sequential matching without feature embedding. With this speed-up, the recognition performances on the two datasets degraded 5.8% and 2.4%, respectively. We observe that the performance of the proposed algorithm is scalable with the database size without sacrificing much accuracy.

- The prediction of the performance of a biometrics system is an important consideration in the real world applications. By modeling cumulative match characteristic (CMC) curve as a binomial distribution, the ear recognition performance can be predicted on a larger gallery. The performance prediction model showed the scalability of the proposed ear biometrics system with increased database size.

In summary, the research presented in this book is focused on designing an automatic human identification system using 3D ear biometrics. The experimental results on the two large datasets show that ear biometrics has the potential to be used in the real-world applications to identify/authenticate humans by their ears.

Ear biometrics can be used in both the low and high security applications and in combination with other biometrics such as face. With the decreasing cost (few thousand dollars) and size of a 3D scanner and the increased performance, we believe that 3D ear biometrics will be highly useful in many real-world applications in the future.

9.2 Future Work

Although the algorithms we have developed achieved a good performance in 3D ear recognition, we believe that there are still some problems that need to be worked on to make automatic ear recognition system more effective and efficient in real world applications. In the following, we list the possible directions, which can improve the performance of our algorithms:

- Currently we used both color and range images for ear detection but only used 3D range image for ear recognition. Since the Minolta sensor provides us a range image and a registered color image, incorporating the color information into the recognition system can further improve the recognition performance.
- We introduced a new integrated local surface patch representation for matching 3D ears and we achieved good recognition performance on the two large datasets. However the LSP representation

only used the geometric information. It is possible to combine it with other appreance-based compact representations.

- We achieved a sublinear time complexity with respect to the size of database and the average time per query was reduced by a factor of 6. For large scale identification applications further improvement and efficient indexing techniques are desirable.

- Ear biometrics (3D and/or 2D) can be combined with (3D and/or 2D) face and side face for robust human recognition.

- It is possible to use the infrared images of ears to overcome the problem of occlusion of the ear by hair.

- Recent work in acoustic recognition allows one to determine the impulse response of an ear [113]. It is possible to combine shape-based ear recognition presented in this book with the acoustic recognition of ear [113] so as to develop an extremely fool-proof system for recognizing a live individual.

- It is possible to develop new volume based features for 3D ear recognition. Thus, one can obtain multiple representations for ear recognition.

References

1. H. Chen and B. Bhanu, "Human ear recognition in 3D," *IEEE Trans. Pattern Analysis and Machine Intelligence*, vol. 29, no. 4, pp. 718–737, 2007.
2. P. Yan and K. W. Bowyer, "Biometric recognition using 3D ear shape," *IEEE Trans. Pattern Analysis and Machine Intelligence*, vol. 29, no. 8, pp. 1297–1308, 2007.
3. A.E. Johnson and M. Hebert, "Using spin images for efficient object recognition in cluttered 3D scenes," *IEEE Trans. Pattern Analysis and Machine Intelligence*, vol. 21, no. 5, pp. 433–449, 1999.
4. S.R. Correa and L.G Shapiro, "A new signature-based method for efficient 3-D object recognition," *Proc. IEEE Conf. Computer Vision and Pattern Recognition*, vol. 1, pp. 769–776, 2001.
5. A. Bertillon, *La phtotgraphie judiciaire, avec un appendice sur la classification et l'identification anthropometriques*, Gauthier-Villars, Paris, 1890.
6. D.J. Hurley, B. Arbab-Zavar, and M.S. Nixon, "The ear as a biometric," *in A. Jain, P. Flynn, A. Ross, Handbook of Biometrics, Springer*, 2007.
7. A.K. Jain, R. Bolle, and S. Pankanti, Eds., *Biometrics: Personal Identification in Network Society*, Kluwer Academic, 1999.
8. A. Iannarelli, *Ear Identification*, Forensic Identification Series. Paramont Publishing Company, 1989.
9. M. Burge and W. Burger, "Ear biometrics in computer vision," *Proc. Int. Conf. on Pattern Recognition*, vol. 2, pp. 822–826, 2000.
10. D.J. Hurley, M.S. Nixon, and J.N. Carter, "Force field feature extraction for ear biometrics," *Computer Vision and Image Understanding*, vol. 98, no. 3, pp. 491–512, 2005.
11. K. Chang, K. W. Bowyer, S. Sarkar, and B. Victor, "Comparison and combination of ear and face images in appearance-based biometrics," *IEEE Trans. Pattern Analysis and Machine Intelligence*, vol. 25, no. 9, pp. 1160–1165, 2003.
12. B. Bhanu and H. Chen, "Human ear recognition in 3D," *Proc. Workshop on Multimodal User Authentication*, pp. 91–98, 2003.
13. H. Chen and B. Bhanu, "Contour matching for 3D ear recognition," *Proc. 7th IEEE Workshops on Application of Computer Vision*, vol. 1, pp. 123–128, 2005.
14. P. Yan and K. W. Bowyer, "Multi-biometrics 2D and 3D ear recognition," *Proc. Audio and Video Based Biometric Person Authentication*, pp. 503–512, 2005.
15. P. Yan and K. W. Bowyer, "Empirical evaluation of advanced ear biometrics," *Proc. IEEE Conf. Computer Vision and Pattern Recognition Workshop on Empirical Evaluation Methods in Computer Vision*, 2005.

16. P. Yan and K. W. Bowyer, "Ear biometrics using 2D and 3D images," *Proc. IEEE Conf. Computer Vision and Pattern Recognition Workshop on Advanced 3D Imaging for Safety and Security*, 2005.

17. P. Yan and K. W. Bowyer, "ICP-based approaches for 3D ear recognition," *Proc. SPIE Conf. on Biometric Technology for Human Identification*, pp. 282–291, 2005.

18. P. Yan and K. W. Bowyer, "A fast algorithm for ICP-based 3D shape biometrics," *Proc. IEEE Workshop on Automatic Identification Advanced Technologies*, pp. 213–218, 2005.

19. P. Yan and K. W. Bowyer, "An automatic 3D ear recognition system," *Third International Symposium on 3D Data Processing, Visualization and Transmission*, pp. 213–218, 2006.

20. "State v. David Wayne Kunze court of appeals of washington, division 2. 97 wash.app. 832, 988 p.2d 977," http://forensic-evidence.com/site/ID/ID_Kunze.html, 1999.

21. "Man convicted of murder by earprint is freed," http://www.timesonline.co.uk/tol/news/article1000889.ece, Jan 2004.

22. G.N. Rutty, A. Abbas, and D. Crossling, "Could earprint identification be compterised? an illustrated proof of concept paper," *International Journal of Legal Medicine*, vol. 119, no. 6, pp. 335–343, 2005.

23. L. Meijermana, S. Shollb, F. De Contic, M. Giaconc, G. van der Lugtd, A. Drusinic, P. Vanezis, and G. Maata, "Exploratory study on classification and individualisation of earprints," *Forensic Science International*, vol. 140, pp. 91–99, 2004.

24. D.J. Hurley, M.S. Nixon, and J.N. Carter, "Automatic ear recognition by force field transformations," *IEE Colloquium on Visual Biometrics*, pp. 7/1 –7/5, 2000.

25. B. Victor, K. Bowyer, and S. Sarkar, "An evaluation of face and ear biometrics," *Proc. Int. Conf. on Pattern Recognition*, vol. 1, pp. 429–432, 2002.

26. M. Abdel-Mottaleb and J. Zhou, "Human ear recognition from face profile images," *Proc. Int. Conf. on Advances in Biometrics*, pp. 786–792, 2006.

27. L. Yuan, Z. Mu, and Y. Liu, "Multimodal recognition using face profile and ear," *1st International Symposium on Systems and Control in Aerospace and Astronautics*, pp. 887–891, 2006.

28. Z. Mu, L. Yuan, Z. Xu, D. Xi, and S. Qi, "Shape and structural feature based ear recognition," *Advances in Biometric Person Authentication, 5th Chinese Conference on Biometric Recognition, SINOBIOMETRICS 2004*, pp. 663–670, 2004.

29. L. Yuan, Z. Mu, Y. Zhang, and K. Lie, "Ear recognition using improved non-negative matrix factorization," *Proc. Int. Conf. on Pattern Recognition*, vol. 4, pp. 501–504, 2006.

30. A. F. Abate, M. Nappi, D. Riccio, and S. Ricciardi, "Ear recognition by means of a rotation invariant descriptor," *Proc. Int. Conf. on Pattern Recognition*, vol. 4, pp. 437–440, 2006.

31. H. Zhang, Z. Mu, W. Qu, L. Liu, and C. Zhang, "A novel approach for ear recognition based on ICA and RBF network," *Proc. Int. Conf. on Machine Learning and Cybernetics*, vol. 7, pp. 4511–4515, 2005.

32. M. Choras, "Further developments in geometrical algorithms for ear biometrics," *Proc. on Articulated Motion and Deformable Objects*, pp. 58–67, 2006.

33. K.H. Pun and Y.S. Moon, "Recent advances in ear biometrics," *Proc. Int. Conf. on Automatic Face and Gesture Recognition*, pp. 164–169, 2004.

34. P. Yan, *Ear Biometrics in Human Identification*, Ph.D. thesis, Department of Computer Science and Engineering, University of Notre Dame, 2006.

35. H. Chen and B. Bhanu, "Human ear detection from side face range images," *Proc. Int. Conf. on Pattern Recognition*, vol. 3, pp. 574–577, 2004.

36. H. Chen and B. Bhanu, "Shape model-based 3D ear detection from side face range images," *Proc. IEEE Conf. Computer Vision and Pattern Recognition Workshop on Advanced 3D Imaging for Safety and Security*, 2005.

37. C. Boehnen and T. Russ, "A fast multi-modal approach to facial feature detection," *Proc. 7th IEEE Workshops on Application of Computer Vision*, vol. 1, pp. 135–142, 2005.

38. F. Tsalakanidou, S. Malasiotis, and M. G. Strintzis, "Face localization and authentication using color and depth images," *IEEE Trans. on Image Processing*, vol. 14, no. 2, pp. 152–168, 2005.

39. X. Lu, D. Colbry, and A. K. Jain, "Three-dimensional model based face recognition," *Proc. Int. Conf. on Pattern Recognition*, vol. 1, pp. 362–366, 2004.

40. J. C. Lee and E. Milios, "Matching range images of human faces," *Proc. Int. Conf. on Computer Vision*, pp. 722–726, 1990.

41. G. G. Gordon, "Face recognition based on depth and curvature features," *Proc. IEEE Conf. Computer Vision and Pattern Recognition*, pp. 808–810, 1992.

42. C. S. Chua, F. Han, and Y. Ho, "3D human face recognition using point signatures," *Proc. Int. Conf. on Automatic Face and Gesture Recognition*, pp. 233–238, 2000.

43. A. Bronstein, M. Bronstein, and R. Kimmel, "Expression-invariant 3D face recognition," *Proc. Audio and Video Based Biometric Person Authentication*, pp. 62–70, 2003.

44. K. Chang, Kevin W. Bowyer, and Patrick Flynn, "Multi-modal 2D and 3D biometrics for face recognition," *IEEE Int. Workshop on Analysis and Modeling of Faces and Gestures*, pp. 187–194, 2003.

45. K. Chang, K. W. Bowyer, and P. Flynn, "An evaluation of multi-modal 2D+3D face biometrics," *IEEE Trans. Pattern Analysis and Machine Intelligence*, vol. 27, no. 4, pp. 619–624, 2005.

46. X. Lu and A. K. Jain, "Integrating range and texture information for 3D face recognition," *Proc. 7th IEEE Workshops on Application of Computer Vision*, vol. 1, pp. 156–163, 2005.

47. P. Yan and K. W. Bowyer, "A fast algorithm for ICP-based 3D shape biometrics," *Proc. IEEE Workshop on Automatic Identification Advanced Technologies*, pp. 213–218, 2005.

48. B. Bhanu, "Representation and shape matching of 3-D objects," *IEEE Trans. Pattern Analysis and Machine Intelligence*, vol. 6, no. 3, pp. 340–351, 1984.

49. M. Suk and S. Bhandarkar, *Three-Dimensional Object Recognition from Range Images*, Springer-Verlag, 1992.

50. B. Bhanu and C.C. Ho, "CAD-based 3D object representations for robot vision," *IEEE Computer*, vol. 20, no. 8, pp. 19–35, 1987.

51. R. J. Campbell and P. J. Flynn, "A survey of free-form object representation and recognition techniques," *Computer Vision and Image Image Understanding*, vol. 81, pp. 166–210, 2001.

52. F. Stein and G. Medioni, "Structural indexing: efficient 3-D object recognition," *IEEE Trans. Pattern Analysis and Machine Intelligence*, vol. 14, no. 2, pp. 125–145, 1992.

53. C.S. Chua and R. Jarvis, "Point signatures: A new representation for 3D object recognition," *Proc. International Journal of Computer Vision*, vol. 25, no. 1, pp. 63–85, 1997.

54. S. M. Yamany and A. A. Farag, "Free-form surface registration using surface signatures," *Proc. Int. Conf. on Computer Vision*, vol. 2, pp. 1098–1104, 1999.

55. D. Zhang and M. Hebert, "Harmonic maps and their applications in surface matching," *Proc. IEEE Conf. Computer Vision and Pattern Recognition*, vol. 2, pp. 524–530, 1999.

56. Y. Sun and M. A. Abidi, "Surface matching by 3D point's fingerprint," *Proc. Int. Conf. on Computer Vision*, vol. 2, pp. 263–269, 2001.

57. H. Chen and B. Bhanu, "3D free-form object recognition in range images using local surface patches," *Proc. Int. Conf. on Pattern Recognition*, vol. 3, pp. 136–139, 2004.

58. F. Mokhtarian, N. Khalili, and P. Yuen, "Multi-scale free-form 3D object recognition using 3D models," *Image and Vision Computing*, vol. 19, pp. 271–281, 2001.

59. J. H. Yi and D. M. Chelberg, "Model-based 3D object recognition using Bayesian indexing," *Computer Vision and Image Understanding*, vol. 69, no. 1, pp. 87–105, 1998.

60. C. Dorai and A.K. Jain, "COSMOS-a representation scheme for free-form surfaces," *Proc. Int. Conf. on Computer Vision*, pp. 1024–1029, 1995.

61. P.J. Flynn and A.K. Jain, "On reliable curvature estimation," *Proc. IEEE Conf. Computer Vision and Pattern Recognition*, pp. 110–116, 1989.

62. B. Schiele and J.L. Crowley, "Recognition without correspondence using multidimensional receptive field histograms," *International Journal of Computer Vision*, vol. 36, no. 1, pp. 31–50, 2000.

63. P.J. Besl and N. D. Mckay, "A method of registration of 3-D shapes," *IEEE Trans. Pattern Analysis and Machine Intelligence*, vol. 14, no. 2, pp. 239–256, 1992.

64. G. Turk and M. Levoy, "Zippered polygon meshes from range images," *Proceedings of Conf. on Computer Graphics and Interactive Techniques*, pp. 311–318, 1994.

65. M. J. Jones and J. M. Rehg, "Statistical color models with application to skin detection," *International Journal of Computer Vision*, vol. 46, no. 1, pp. 81–96, 2002.

66. T. F. Cootes, D. Cooper, C. J. Taylor, and J. Graham, "Active shape models - their training and application," *Computer Vision and Image Understanding*, vol. 61, no. 1, pp. 38–59, 1995.

67. C. S. Chen, Y. P. Hung, and J. B. Cheng, "RANSAC-based DARCES: A new approach to fast automatic registration of partially overlapping range images," *IEEE Trans. Pattern Analysis and Machine Intelligence*, vol. 21, no. 11, pp. 1229–1234, 1999.

68. F. L. Bookstein, "Principal warps: Thin-plate splines and the decomposition of deformations," *IEEE Trans. Pattern Analysis and Machine Intelligence*, vol. 11, no. 6, pp. 567–585, 1989.

69. Y. Chen and G. Medioni, "Object modelling by registration of multiple range images," *Image and Vision Computing*, vol. 10, no. 3, pp. 145–155, 1992.

70. Z. Zhang, "Iterative point matching for registration of free-form curves and surfaces," *International Journal of Computer Vision*, vol. 13, no. 2, pp. 119–152, 1994.

71. S. Rusinkiewicz and M. Levoy, "Efficient variants of the ICP algorithm," *Proc. Int. Conf. on 3-D Digital Imaging and Modeling*, pp. 145–152, 2001.

72. H. Chui and A. Rangaraian, "A new algorithm for non-rigid point matching," *Proc. IEEE Conf. Computer Vision and Pattern Recognition*, vol. 2, pp. 44–51, 2000.

73. S. Wang, T. Kubota, and T. Richardson, "Shape correspondence through landmark sliding," *Proc. IEEE Conf. Computer Vision and Pattern Recognition*, vol. 1, pp. 143–150, 2004.

74. J. Lim and M. H. Yang, "A direct method for modeling non-rigid motion with thin plate spline," *Proc. IEEE Conf. Computer Vision and Pattern Recognition*, vol. 1, pp. 196–202, 2005.

75. M. Kass, A. Witkin, and D. Terzopoulos, "Snakes: active contour models," *International Journal of Computer Vision*, vol. 1, no. 14, pp. 321–331, 1988.

76. B.K.P. Horn, "Close-form solution of absolute orientation using unit quaternions," *Journal of the Optical Society of America*, vol. 4, no. 4, pp. 629–642, 1987.

77. C. Dorai and A.K. Jain, "COSMOS-A representation scheme for 3D free-form objects," *IEEE Trans. Pattern Analysis and Machine Intelligence*, vol. 19, no. 10, pp. 1115–1130, 1997.

78. D. Huber, *Automatic Three-Dimensional Modeling from Reality*, Ph.D. thesis, The Robotics Institute, Carnegie Mellon University, 2002.

79. A. S. Mian, M. Bennamoun, and R. Owens, "A novel representation and feature matching algorithm for automatic pairwise registration of range images," *International Journal of Computer Vision*, vol. 66, no. 1, pp. 19–40, 2006.

80. A. Frome, D. Huber, R. Kolluri, T. Bulow, and J. Malik, "Recognizing objects in range data using regional point descriptors," *Proc. European Conference on Computer Vision*, pp. 224–237, 2004.

81. C. Kotropoulos, A. Tefas, and I. Pitas, "Frontal face authentication using discriminating grids with morphological feature vectors," *IEEE Trans. on Multimedia*, vol. 2, no. 1, pp. 14–26, 2000.

82. W. Shen, M. Surette, and R. Khanna, "Evaluation of automated biometric-based identification and verification systems," *Proc. of the IEEE*, vol. 85, no. 9, pp. 1464–1478, 1997.

83. H. Chen and B. Bhanu, "3D free-form object recognition in range images using local surface patches," *Pattern Recognition Letters*, vol. 28, no. 10, pp. 1252–1262, 2007.

84. B. Matei, Y. Shan, H. Sawhney, Y. Tan, R. Kumar, D. Huber, and M. Hebert, "Rapid object indexing using locality sensitive hashing and joint 3D-signature space estimation," *IEEE Trans. Pattern Analysis and Machine Intelligence*, vol. 28, no. 7, pp. 1111–1126, 2006.

85. A. Gionis, P. Indyk, and R. Motwani, "Similarity search in high dimensions via hashing," *Proc. 25th Int'l Conf. Very Large DataBases*, pp. 518–529, 1999.

86. Meinard Muller, Tido Roder, and Michael Clausen, "Efficient content-based retrieval of motion capture data," *Proc. ACM SIGGRAPH*, pp. 677–685, 2005.

87. Y. Rubner, C. Tomasi, and L. J. Guibas, "A metric for distributions with applications to image databases," *Proc. Int. Conf. on Computer Vision*, pp. 59–66, 1998.

88. S. Roweis and L. Saul, "Nonlinear dimensionality reduction by locally linear embedding," *Science*, vol. 290, pp. 2323–2326, 2000.

89. F. Young and R. Hamer, *Multidimensional Scaling: History, Theory and Applications*, Lawrence Erlbaum Associates, 1987.

90. J. Tenenbaum, V. Silva, and J. Langford, "A global geometric framework for nonlinear dimensionality reduction," *Science*, vol. 290, pp. 2319–2323, 2000.

91. G. Hjaltason and H. Samet, "Properties of embedding methods for similarity searching in metric spaces," *IEEE Trans. Pattern Analysis and Machine Intelligence*, vol. 25, no. 5, pp. 530–549, 2003.

92. C. Faloutsos and K. Lin, "FastMap: a fast algorithm for indexing, data-mining and visualization of traditional and multimedia datasets," *Proc. of the ACM SIGMOD International Conference on Management of Data*, pp. 163–174, 1995.

93. X. Wang, J. Wang, K. Lin, D. Shasha, B. Shapiro, and K. Zhang, "An index structure for data mining and clustering," *Knowledge and Information Systems*, vol. 2, no. 2, pp. 161–184, 2000.

94. V. Athitsos, J. Alon, S. Sclaroff, and G. Kollios, "BoostMap: A method for efficient approximate similarity rankings," *Proc. IEEE Conf. Computer Vision and Pattern Recognition*, vol. 2, pp. 268–275, 2004.

95. T. Joachims, "Optimizing search engines using clickthrough data," *Proc. the ACM Conference on Knowledge Discovery and Data Mining*, pp. 133–142, 2002.

96. R. Wang and B. Bhanu, "Learning models for predicting recognition performance," *Proc. Int. Conf. on Computer Vision*, pp. 1613–1618, 2005.

97. R. Wang and B. Bhanu, "Predicting fingerprint biometrics performance from a small gallery," *Pattern Recognition Letters*, vol. 28, no. 1, pp. 40–48, 2007.

98. X. Tan and B. Bhanu, "On the fundamental performance for fingerprint matching," *Proc. IEEE Conf. Computer Vision and Pattern Recognition*, vol. 2, pp. 499–504, 2003.

99. S. Pankanti, S. Prabhakar, and A.K. Jain, "On the individuality of fingerprints," *IEEE Trans. Pattern Anal. Mach. Intell.*, vol. 24, no. 8, pp. 1010–1025, 2002.

100. A. Y. Johnson, J. Sun, and A. F. Boick, "Predicting large population data cumulative match characteristic performance from small population data," *Audio and Video Based Biometric Person Authentication*, pp. 821–829, 2003.

101. J. L. Wayman, "Error-rate equations for the general biometric system," *IEEE Robotics & Automation Magazine*, vol. 6, no. 1, pp. 35–48, 1999.

102. J. Daugman, "The importance of being random: statistical principles of iris recognition," *Pattern Recognition*, vol. 36, no. 2, pp. 279–291, 2003.

103. A. Y. Johnson, J. Sun, and A. F. Boick, "Using similarity scores from a small gallery to estimate recognition performance for large galleries," *IEEE Int. Workshop on Analysis and Modeling of Faces and Gestures*, pp. 100–103, 2003.

104. P. Grother and P. J. Phillips, "Models of large population recognition performance," *Proc. IEEE Conf. Computer Vision and Pattern Recognition*, vol. 2, pp. 68–75, 2004.

105. H. Chen, B. Bhanu, and R. Wang, "Performance evaluation and prediction for 3D ear recognition," *Proc. Audio and Video Based Biometric Person Authentication*, pp. 748–757, 2005.

106. P.J. Besl and R.C. Jain, "Segmentation through variable-order surface fitting," *IEEE Trans. Pattern Analysis and Machine Intelligence*, vol. 10, no. 2, pp. 167–192, 1988.

107. B. Bhanu and L.A. Nuttall, "Recognition of 3-D objects in range images using a butterfly multiprocessor," *Pattern Recognition*, vol. 22, no. 1, pp. 49–64, 1989.

108. S. Belongie, J. Malik, and J. Puzicha, "Shape matching and object recognition using shape contexts," *IEEE Trans. Pattern Analysis and Machine Intelligence*, vol. 24, no. 24, pp. 509–522, 2002.

109. H. Guo, A. Rangarajan, S. Joshi, and L. Younes, "Non-rigid registration of shapes via diffeomorphic point matching," *IEEE International Symposium on Biomedical Imaging: Macro to Nano*, vol. 1, pp. 924–927, 2004.

110. N. Paragios, M. Rousson, and V. Ramesh, "Non-rigid registration using distance functions," *Computer Vision and Image Understanding*, vol. 89, pp. 142–165, 2003.

111. Y. Zheng and D. Doermann, "Robust point matching for two-dimensional nonrigid shapes," *Proc. Int. Conf. on Computer Vision*, vol. 1, pp. 561–566, 2005.

112. H. Chen and B. Bhanu, "Global-to-local non-rigid shape registration," *Proc. Int. Conf. on Pattern Recognition*, vol. 4, pp. 57–60, 2006.

113. A. H. M. Akkermans, T. A. M. Kevenaar, and D. W. E. Schobben, "Acoustic ear recognition for person identification," *Proc. IEEE Workshop on Automatic Identification Advanced Technologies*, pp. 219–223, 2005.

Index